YOU GOTTA PLAY TO WIN!

the
ALL-STAR
★ SALES BOOK ★

GET IN THE GAME,
BOOST YOUR NUMBERS,
AND EARN THE BIG BUCKS

BILLY COX

GREENLEAF
BOOK GROUP PRESS

Published by Greenleaf Book Group Press
4425 S. Mo Pac Expy., Suite 600
Austin, TX 78735

Distributed by Greenleaf Book Group LP

For ordering information or special discounts for bulk purchases, please contact Greenleaf Book Group LP at 4425 S. Mo Pac Expy., Suite 600, Austin, TX 78735, (512) 891-6100.

Design and composition by Greenleaf Book Group LP
Cover design by Greenleaf Book Group LP

Publisher's Cataloging-In-Publication Data
(Prepared by The Donohue Group, Inc.)

Cox, Billy, 1967-
  The all-star sales book : get in the game, boost your numbers, and earn the big bucks / Billy Cox.—1st ed.

    p. ; cm.
  At head of title: You gotta play to win!
  Includes index.
  ISBN: 978-1-929774-48-7
1. Selling. 2. Sales personnel. 3. Success in business. I. Title. II. Title: You gotta play to win!
HF5438.25 .C69 2008
658.85

Printed in the United States of America on acid-free paper

13 12 11 10 09 08   10 9 8 7 6 5 4 3 2 1

First Edition

DEDICATION

I dedicate this book to Zig Ziglar. Other than my parents and God, there is no one individual who has impacted my life more than Zig Ziglar. When I was a struggling salesperson flat broke and behind on my bills, it was Ziglar audios that kept me focused and believing I could make it.

When my young daughter passed away, it was Ziglar's teachings that inspired me and my family to pick ourselves up and keep our faith. Five years ago, I was out of shape and my energy level was low. Once again, I used Ziglar's advice to get started on a regular exercise program and now I am in the best shape of my life. It was Zig's influence that inspired me to write books and to share my life's experiences through books, audio, and professional speaking.

Ziglar taught me some key principles like "You can have everything in life you want if you will just help enough other people get what they want." And that money isn't everything but it is up there with air and oxygen. I also learned that money can buy you a house, but it can't buy you a home, family, joy, health, or love.

Ziglar lives what he teaches and his faith, character, and high moral standards are reflected through every employee at ziglar.com.

His message has influenced millions of individuals around the globe and they have influenced me. For that, I am forever grateful. Thanks Zig.

CONTENTS

MY MESSAGE TO YOU

Throughout my career I have read many books that have dramatically increased my income and positively changed my life. I have also started reading many books I never finished because I couldn't relate to them or they were too long and cumbersome. This book is different. It is fast paced and easy to read, short and to the point.

If you are reading this book, it is because you are a winner. It doesn't matter if you are a veteran or a rookie, I know that winners never rest on their laurels. They constantly look for new ways to improve their performance while remaining true to the basic fundamentals that brought them to the game. So read this book from start to finish because the information inside can make a lasting impact on your performance.

And remember, winners commit themselves to helping those around them win. So, enjoy the book and make the most of it by sharing the ideas and strategies with everyone on your team.

★ INTRODUCTION ★

IN THE GAME OF LIFE, business, and sales, there are no time-outs, no overtimes. You only get one chance to play the game. The question you gotta ask yourself is, At what level do I want to play—do I want to wait on the sidelines or do I want to win?

If you really want to win, if you want to be an all-star, you gotta get in the game!

The all-stars are the elite performers who have earned the right to play with the very best. In this book, I call them all-stars, but others call them superstars, champions, leaders, top performers, or high achievers. You can call them anything you want, but one thing is for sure . . . they are winners. And when the game is on the line, they consistently step up to the plate and knock the ball out of the park.

These franchise players exist in every company and on every sales team. They are the ones who take initiative, make things happen, and do whatever it takes to help their team win. They also back the action up with consistency year after year. Yes, even winners lose a game or two, but the all-stars constantly pick themselves up, learn from their mistakes, and come back stronger than ever before.

Although I've never made a dime as a professional athlete, I have discovered there are many similarities between success in sports and success in life, business, and sales in general. In sports, it's not uncommon for two athletes with the same talents, skills, and abilities to perform at dramatically different levels. One might be an average player while the other is an all-star.

The same is true in sales. Oftentimes someone will sell twice as much or make many times the income of others who have the same basic talents and skills and work in the same territory. They may also live happier, more successful, and more productive lives. In fact, the all-stars in life and business frequently have less education and experience than the average performers, and yet they achieve extraordinary levels of success. Why?

Early in my life I learned how small improvements in key areas of your sales approach and practices can lead to enormous differences in results. What this means is that very slight differences are what separate the all-stars from the average performers.

You see, anybody can succeed sometimes, but winning is not a sometime thing—it's an all the time thing. The all-stars win because they consistently do the little things that the average performers don't. They practice more hours than the average performers, they strive harder than the average performers, and they do the small things over and over again until they achieve winning results.

I also learned that all-stars are coachable. They are students of the game and are always looking for ways to take their game (or performance) to the next level. As a result, they are constantly raising their bar by raising their standards.

Many people play the game but never win. People fail because they don't do the little things that will give them the edge it takes to win. As a result, they're playing to lose without even realizing it.

You may be wondering, Why should I want to get in the game? Why should I put forth all this effort to be an all-star? What's the payoff for me? Those are fair questions, and before you embark on any journey (or game) you should know where it can take you. When you achieve all-star success, the payoff is big—big fun, big joy, big competition, big recognition, big championships, big success, and yes, *BIG BUCKS*.

No, money is not everything and focusing on money at all costs is a recipe for disaster. But, when you play to win and you do it the right way, the big money comes as a natural part of the process. Most importantly, you get to experience all the great things with family, friends, and team mates that money can't buy. Yes, being an all-star truly is a win-win for everyone involved.

Read this book in its entirety and it will show you how to play, compete, and succeed at the highest level. The strategies and techniques are tried and true—they work. They have worked in my life, and I have seen them work time and time again in the lives of countless others.

To get the full effect of this book, you must first understand that when I started out in sales, I was very young, inexperienced, and flat broke. Over a period of fifteen years, I worked my way to the top of every sales and management position, eventually becoming president and chief operating officer of a highly successful international sales-driven company.

Throughout this journey, I made many mistakes and learned many valuable lessons, experienced many triumphs and faced much adversity. I can tell you that all winners have scars. And, no matter what level of success you have achieved before, your past doesn't have to dictate your future. High achievers in all walks of life have ups and downs, victories and setbacks. Learning how others have turned their setbacks into comebacks can inspire you to do the small things that will give you the edge it takes to win.

As you read this book, you'll notice how much I use the phrase *you gotta*. Though it may not be proper grammar, it is a powerful phrase that inspires action. All of us have a list of things we should do: we should make those extra sales calls, we should start mentoring others, we should make the necessary changes to get that next promotion. To succeed at all-star levels *you gotta* turn your shoulds, coulds, woulds, mights, and maybes into action-oriented results if you want to achieve lasting success.

So, when you come across a *you gotta*, pay special attention and read the text that follows very carefully—it identifies the crucial steps you gotta take to succeed at the highest level. When you learn and apply these principles, you will quickly rise to the top and your future will be unlimited.

Inside of you there *is* a champion. You *already* have the unlimited potential to play your game at any level you choose. You can sit on the sidelines and watch others win, or you can jump in and play with strength, purpose, passion, and power. You can be a spectator, or you can be an all-star.

My hope is that by reading this book, you will set specific goals and stretch yourself. I hope you're willing to discipline yourself. I hope you want to compete and that you will develop a burning desire to win. I hope you will make the decision to get off the bench and get in the game.

★ CHAPTER 1 ★

YOU GOTTA GET IN THE GAME

I'VE NEVER SEEN ANYONE make a shot from the bench or catch a touchdown from the sideline. I've never seen a top producer, a top performer sit around waiting for someone to call and buy his or her products or services. In order to have any chance at winning, you gotta get off the bench and get in the game!

> **I can't accept not trying.**
> **—Michael Jordan, National Basketball Association Hall of Famer**

Star athletes can't stand to sit. It doesn't matter if the team is twenty points ahead or twenty points behind; the all-stars want to be part of the action. That's why they're all-stars. An all-star athlete can't wait for the next play, and an all-star salesperson can't wait to give the next presentation or close the next sale. True all-stars take the initiative to get in the game; they make things happen.

You can't sit on the bench and be an all-star. There are plenty of benchwarmers. You gotta want to be in the game! You gotta want it with an unstoppable, driving desire!

YOU GOTTA MAKE A DECISION

If you want to get in the game, the first thing you gotta do is make a decision. A decision is a definite, conscious choice to do something. People make decisions—to improve their performance, to increase their numbers, to get to the next level—every day, but most of them are made without putting much thought or commitment behind the decisions.

Through my experiences, I've discovered that the top performers always make a conscious, committed decision to be the best. They leave themselves no outs. They say to themselves, "No matter what, I'm going to do it. That's it. Period." Making a conscious decision to do something is one of the defining differences between people who achieve great results and those who achieve mediocre results. They both have more or less the same abilities and opportunities, so it comes down to who is willing to make a decision and take action.

The first major turning point in my career involved a decision. When I started in sales, I was seventeen years old, fresh out of high school, and flat broke. So, I decided I would try sales part-time to make a little extra money. But I wasn't committed; I wasn't in the game. I looked at sales only as a way to make some money, and as a result, my career was like a roller coaster—there were months I rose to the top and months I plunged to the bottom.

> **Destiny is not a matter of chance; it is a matter of choice.**
>
> **—William Jennings Bryan**
> **speaker, lawyer, and politician**

I remember one month specifically. It was the worst month of my sales career. I made one sale for a $100 commission, but it cost me $500 in expenses to make that sale! By the end of the month, I was discouraged and had lost my confidence. I was sick and tired of the situation I had created and seemed stuck in. I was tired of my income—or rather, lack of income—tired of borrowing money from my parents, tired of the car I drove, and tired of my lackadaisical efforts and work habits.

I started to think I wasn't cut out for sales and began looking for a different job. But I soon realized that in any job, I would still have to show up, give my best, and work hard if I wanted to be a top money earner.

Then I thought about some of the salespeople I knew who were making lots of money and having the time of their lives. I also remembered how much money I'd made and how much fun I'd had during the few times I was truly committed. I realized I enjoyed sales, and I felt there was nothing else that

offered me the freedom, excitement, and opportunity that
sales did.

That was the day I made the decision that I was going to
do whatever it took to be a top producer.

That was over twenty years ago, and I can still feel the
power of that moment. I made a definite, conscious choice to
get off the bench. I still had a lot to learn, but I decided I was
willing to do whatever was necessary to make it to the top.

**I made a definite, conscious
choice to get off the bench.**

Over the next few years, I had many ups and downs, but
for the most part, my sales career took a hard turn for the
better. I learned a lot, won many awards and competitions,
and achieved top honors as a salesperson. I was on the fast
track to the top . . . or so I thought.

Eventually, the awards and honors weren't enough. I
needed a new challenge, and I knew exactly what that challenge was: I wanted to start my own sales office. And not
only did I want my own office, I wanted to build a team that
could become number one in the nation. So I made a decision
to do it.

I realized that only one factor determined my success—me.

At this point in my life, I was twenty years old. I had recently met my future bride, Susan, and she supported my decision. We set a date, made the arrangements, and with a lot of help and support, started our new office and our new life together. But after only a few months, I found out that running my own business wasn't as easy as I thought it would be. And to make matters worse, I wasn't working as hard as I should have been. I had gotten a little lazy and was trying to play "executive." In my mind, I had made it to the top.

Suddenly, we two newlyweds, with a new business and a baby on the way, found ourselves with no money and behind on our bills. For the first time since my "one sale, $100 month," I was struggling again. The reality of the situation didn't completely set in until my car disappeared. I thought someone had stolen it, so I immediately called the police. The first thing they asked me was if I had made all the payments. It was only then that I realized my car had been repossessed!

This was another turning point in my life. I realized that only one factor determined my success—me. As the saying goes, "If it is to be, it is up to me." So I made a decision to get my car back. Once I committed to that decision, I did what-ever it took to make it happen. I borrowed a car and found a way to make three sales that day, and those three sales gave me enough money to get my car back and pay my rent for the month.

I learned some valuable lessons from that experience. First, never think you've already made it. It's the surest way to the sidelines, because it will make you complacent. Second, when you make a decision and take action, you can change your life. Because I made a decision to get off the bench and take the initiative, I was able to turn a negative situation into something positive in one day's time.

Are you at a turning point in your life? Then make a clear, unequivocal decision to be the best and don't leave yourself any outs. Tell yourself, "I'm going to do it. That's it. Period." The world is full of people who wish their lives were better but have never made the do-or-die decision that leads to stardom.

YOU GOTTA TAKE ACTION

Everything you have (or don't have) today is the result of the actions you've taken (or haven't taken) in the past. Taking action is like putting your car in gear. You can start the car and sit in it all day, but you'll never go anywhere unless you put it in gear and step on the gas pedal. You see, a decision without action is only a good intention, and good intentions pave the road to nowhere. We all have the option to take action and get into the game, but most of us never do it. Why do we put off doing the things we know we should do? There are many reasons, but the most common are simple procrastination, waiting for somebody or something else to make it happen for us, "paralysis of analysis," and fear or lack of confidence.

**You see, a decision
without action is only a
good intention, and
good intentions pave the
road to nowhere.**

My experience has been that people procrastinate for a number of reasons. For example, we convince ourselves that we cannot overcome our challenges. We tell ourselves that it's going to be too difficult, take too much time, cost too much money, or require too many resources. But these beliefs are rarely true. Taking action usually starts with one simple step that isn't difficult, time-consuming, or costly. And even if it does require resources we think we don't have, if it's a priority, we can find the resources to make it happen. We always find the resources for the things we make a priority.

Some people won't take action because they're waiting for the right situation to magically present itself—they are waiting for the best time, the right opportunity, the new product with a big commission. They're looking for a company, a manager, or even a customer to hand them what they want instead of making it happen themselves. Remember this: no one will ever hand you success. Just like with a car, you can wait for success, but you'll never achieve it unless you get in gear and take action.

Then there are people who feel that before they take action they have to analyze the situation—research it, think it over, and discuss it with family, friends, or colleagues. Others say, "Someday, when I have more experience/learn more and become better, then I'll take action." Let me tell you, the road called "someday" leads to a town called "nowhere." These people will never get in the game!

Please don't get me wrong. Talking things over with other successful people is a good idea; analyzing an opportunity is important; learning is critical. But all the education, experience, and advice in the world won't bring you success if you don't take action. There are many geniuses who don't have a dime because they never took action. There are also many multimillionaires who have very little education and much less knowledge than the geniuses because they constantly take action. Analysis sometimes equals paralysis. Don't get bogged down trying to figure it all out ahead of time. I've been in sales for more than half my life, and I'm still learning. Life is a constant learning and growing process. It is vital for you to take action while you're growing, stretching, striving, and learning.

> **Never let the fear of striking out get in your way.**
>
> **—Babe Ruth, Major League Baseball Hall of Famer**

Perhaps the biggest reason people don't take action is a lack of confidence. Confidence is the feeling that you have what it takes to accomplish whatever task you set out to perform. We're all born with some degree of confidence, but as the years go by, our confidence gets squashed. We hear discouraging words like "no," "you're too young," "you're too old," "you're too slow," "you're not smart enough." And if we hear these negative words often enough, we can easily start using them when we talk to ourselves, hurting our confidence even more.

We also lose confidence as we face life's struggles and challenges—personal failures, business failures, bankruptcies, getting fired or laid off, failing to achieve important goals. Some of these situations are within our control while others are not, but they can all negatively affect our confidence. The bottom line is this: most adults struggle with a lack of confidence every day.

So how can you regain this lost self-confidence once again? You gotta take action! Here is a simple formula I use when teaching people how to gain more confidence:

action $\longrightarrow$ results $\longrightarrow$ success $\longrightarrow$ confidence $\longrightarrow$ action

If you will just take action, eventually you will get some results. Lots of positive results will give you some success. Success will create more confidence. Greater confidence will lead to more action, and the cycle will continue. But it all starts with action.

YOU GOTTA PLAY OFFENSE

Let's face it: It's hard to score when you're playing defense. All-stars play defense for one reason—to get back on offense. They do whatever it takes to block the shot, intercept the pass, and get the outs so they can get back to scoring points.

When you're playing offense you are in the game. No, you can't play offense all of the time, but most people spend the majority of their time going back and forth. They take one step forward on offense and two steps backwards on defense. Therefore, they never achieve the results they desire. Why is this?

When you're playing offense you are in the game.

On a scale of 1 to 10 (1 being "things are utterly miserable" and 10 being "things couldn't be more wonderful"), most of us live and perform at around 5 ("things are tolerable"). But 5 is probably the worst place to be. Things aren't great, but they're not awful, either. Maybe we sell just enough to get all the bills paid each month. Maybe we make just enough calls to meet our quota. We have one foot in the game and one on the sidelines. We know we should do more but there isn't enough pain—enough anxiety—to force us into making a change.

Then something happens that pushes us over the edge. The banker calls to tell us we're $3,000 overdrawn on our checking account. Our boss calls us in to tell us we've missed quota for the second month in a row. We reach the point where we're fed up with the situation; enough is enough. We decide we're not going to live this way anymore—not another day, not another minute. Have you ever had one of these moments in your life?

If you've had one of these turning points and you made the decision to make some positive changes and follow through, that's great. But in the long run, that is not how we want to live our professional, or personal, lives. That's living life in reaction, on the defense. Your environment forced you to take action and let go of whatever was keeping you on the bench. When you live in reaction, you're not in control of your life, of your success—life is in control of you.

> **I've always felt it was not up to anyone else to make me give my best.**
> **—Hakeem Olajuwon, National Basketball Association Hall of Famer**

Don't let circumstances dictate the quality of your performance. Don't be satisfied with the status quo. You don't need a lot of complicated ideas to improve your performance to the next level. All you need is one idea that you will use, one idea that can put you on the offense against mediocrity right now. Take control of your future by taking action now. Now is what you can do this day, hour, or moment to move your life forward.

Top salespeople spend most of their time playing offense. In sales, you're playing offense when you are in front of customers or potential customers. The all-star salespeople spend most of their time prospecting, making sales calls, learning more skills, improving existing skills, and producing measurable results.

So, get out of your chair and call a potential customer now. If you can do that, your confidence will soar and you will motivate yourself to make a second, third, or tenth call. It will only be a matter of time before you achieve better results and make more sales. If you will consistently force yourself to take some kind of action now, to play offense, the process will eventually become a habit and your success will grow.

YOU GOTTA TAKE INITIATIVE

Nike has a famous slogan: "Just do it." This simple statement is more profound than most people realize. It reveals one of the great keys to achieving all-star status. You have to just do it—no excuses.

But if your goal is to achieve all-star status, you have to take it one step further. You gotta take initiative. When it comes to sales performance, I believe that initiative is the power to originate something and the drive to finish what you've started. Some people get started but never finish, others have great follow-through when they do get started, but don't initiate enough action to make a difference. When you can initiate and close, you have initiative.

Initiative gives you the power to win, and the power to help others win. It's more than just taking action or playing offense. It's going above and beyond the call of duty. Individuals who take initiative commit themselves to completing their tasks—for their benefit and their team's benefit. By taking initiative, you become successful and ensure the success of your company and team. When you take initiative you do more than just survive, you thrive.

Having the right products and services is important and timing is crucial to the selling process. However, initiative is

**When you can initiate and
close, you have initiative.**

what sets the top salespeople apart from those who are just average. For example, I was recently interested in purchasing a piece of property. The agent I worked with is the number one salesperson in the nation with his company. His office is also ranked twenty-third in the world in sales. He has made over $7 million in commissions in the last five years. I looked at over ten different properties and declined them all.

What impressed me most about my agent was that he was not discouraged by my repeatedly telling him no. He was clearly focused on the end result of finding me a piece of property. During the six months we have been working together, my desire to buy a piece of property has diminished tremendously. However, he's as optimistic as ever that he'll find a piece of property I'll be satisfied with. Every time I have visited him in his office he is selling to people on the telephone or leaving them messages about homes or properties that might interest them. He takes advantage of every lead and works it to its fullest extent with the same energy and enthusiasm no matter how many calls he has made during the day. After experiencing his "sales initiative" firsthand and seeing him in action in his office, I know why he is the top salesperson in the nation. "No" doesn't faze him and he is persistent until he gets the sale. I'm

Remember, decisions always initiate change and eliminate weak justifications and excuses.

confident that I will eventually buy a piece of property from him, and I will continue our business relationship for many years to come. He's in the game, and that's the key to all-star success.

Remember, decisions always initiate change and eliminate weak justifications and excuses. The truth of the matter is, you know deep in your heart it's what you gotta do. So make a decision today to move your performance to a higher level. If you're at a 5, make a decision and take action now to move to a 6 and beyond. To get in the game, focus your attention on the immediate process of making a decision and taking action now. Even if you think you don't know how or you lack confidence, you gotta do it anyway . . . and you gotta do it now!

To be an all-star, you gotta get in the game.

To get in the game, you gotta

- Make a decision
- Take action
- Play offense
- Take initiative

★ CHAPTER 2 ★

YOU GOTTA HAVE A DREAM

ALTHOUGH MOST OF US will never be star athletes or win Olympic gold medals, we can all perform at the top of our own game. But to do that, you gotta have a dream.

A dream is what inspires you to get off the bench and get into the game. Dreams are the big vision of what you would be, do, or have if money and time were no object. To accomplish your dreams *you gotta* turn them into specific goals. Goals are simply dreams with deadlines. They are the targets you strive for and the signposts that move and guide you in the direction of your ultimate dreams. Goals are also a means of "keeping score" so that you can determine if you're winning the game.

> **Champions aren't made in gyms. Champions are made from something they have deep inside them—a desire, a dream, a vision.**
>
> **—Muhammad Ali, former heavyweight boxing champion of the world**

Dreams and goals give you a definiteness of purpose. They help you know where you're going. But they can do more than guide you. As a salesperson, goal setting is without a doubt one of the primary determinants of your income. Salespeople who have dreams and clearly defined goals make 80 percent of the money.

Based on my experiences and observations, I've concluded that at least 90 percent of success derives from having a dream and knowing what you want. When I coach others, I stress that they have to focus on their dreams. If they already have dreams, they almost always need to redefine them and make them bigger. Then I teach them a simple but powerful system for achieving their dreams and goals.

YOU GOTTA KNOW WHERE YOU'RE GOING

People with dreams and goals succeed because of one primary reason: They know where they're going. In any game, you must determine what winning means to you—*you gotta* define success and you also have to determine what it will take to win. Think about it: a marathon runner has to know where the finish line is and the path to get there to win the race. A runner must develop a winning strategy that includes proper training, nutrition, and hydration; pace setting; and overcoming race-day obstacles. A runner must also know when to attempt to overtake the other competitors to get in a position to win. Skiers must know where the finish line is and how fast they need to get there to develop a strategy for winning the race. Hockey players have to know where the goal is before they can navigate around their opponents, anticipate the other players' moves, and get the puck past the goalie.

The same is true for you. You gotta know where you want to go and have a plan or strategy for how to get there. Otherwise, you could end up almost anywhere. The challenge for each of us is defining our destination. Each of us will have our own distinct definition of winning because we are unique in our individual dreams and aspirations. Knowing your destination makes the journey possible. This is how you measure results, keep score, and determine whether you win the game. So, if you don't have any dreams or goals, how will you know if you are succeeding?

**Knowing your destination
makes the journey possible.**

In sales, if you don't identify your goals, you will likely end up sitting on the sidelines, maybe even without a job or money. However, if you laser in on your target, you will see the adjustments you need to make along the way to stay on course and achieve your aspirations.

> **There is no passion to be found in playing small—in settling for a life that is less than what you are capable of living.**
>
> **—Nelson Mandela**

Take the time right now to think about what success means to you. Where do you want to go and how do you want to grow? One way to answer this question is to imagine yourself five, ten, or even twenty years from now. Constantly thinking about your dreams and goals will encourage you to stay the course. Think about how you will feel when you

Where do you want to go and how do you want to grow?

achieve them. Will you feel successful, fulfilled, and happy? Clarity about your future endeavors will help you hit your target with speed and precision. Consider the following questions:

- What do you love most about sales?
- What do you want to achieve more than anything in the world?
- How could you increase your performance so that it will translate into higher income?
- If you achieved your dreams and goals, who would it affect in a positive way?

Getting clear about your definition of success better prepares you to set the goals that will lead you down the path to all-star success.

YOU GOTTA WRITE DOWN YOUR GOALS

I have found that the biggest mistake people make when working toward their dreams and goals is not writing them down. You may have thought a lot about your dreams and goals in the past, but if they're not written down, I'd be willing to bet you're not getting the results you desire. Just thinking about your dreams, even if you do it daily, isn't enough. If you truly want to achieve these things, you gotta get them on paper.

> **Until you commit your goals to paper, you have intentions that are seeds without soil.**
>
> **—Unknown**

One person who taught me a lot about goals is the man who recruited me into sales, Gene Shelton. I learned firsthand from him how vital it is to actually write down your goals. At our weekly sales meetings, Gene would ask us for our goals, and I would tell him what I thought he wanted to hear. If someone gave Gene a goal, I always gave him a bigger one. I thought that was what goal setting was all about.

As much as I promised, I wasn't getting results. So one day, Gene asked me to give him a list of the goals I wanted to accomplish professionally and personally in the next ten years. This forced me to take time to think my goals through and write them down. As I did, my thinking started to change. I got excited, and I began to believe deep inside that I could actually accomplish them.

I gave Gene a copy of the list, and he sealed it in an envelope and put it away in a drawer. About five years later, he found that envelope and opened it. To our mutual surprise, every goal I had written down had been accomplished! The amazing thing about this story is, at the time I wrote those goals, I was living in a two-bedroom apartment, behind on my rent payments, and dead broke. Five years later, I had a new home, a new car, and was financially free—and these were the exact goals I had written down and given to Gene.

Writing down my goals gave me clarity because it forced me to define and articulate my dreams. But the power of goal setting is not unique to my situation. According to Zig Ziglar, the University of California at Los Angeles (UCLA) conducted a study on goal setting that focused on people who attended the Peter Lowe Success Seminars. The study included psychiatrists, truck drivers, civil service workers, salespeople, and professors. Those with a balanced, written goals program earned twice as much as those without one: an average of $7,401 a month compared to $3,397 a month. The study also found that those with goals were happier, healthier, and got along better with family members. Imagine the impact a consistent goal-setting program could have on your career, your business, and your finances!

YOU GOTTA HAVE A STRATEGY

We have all heard the old saying, "Success is a journey, not a destination." The reason old clichés like this stand the test of time is because they are true. Knowing what you want is not enough, because the path you take to get there is what will ultimately define your success.

The key to creating a proper strategy is setting short-term goals that will lead you to your ultimate destination. You can't

Many people don't set goals because they can't see themselves actually attaining them.

say, "I want to be a millionaire in seven years," and not think about some of the steps you need to take to achieve that level of success. Many people don't set goals because they can't see themselves actually attaining them. Their excuse is: "I can't see myself as the vice president of sales." That's okay! Can you see yourself as a regional head of sales? If not, can you see yourself as the leader of your sales team? Or, if you didn't make your quota last quarter, can you see yourself making quota next quarter and exceeding it next year? After you achieve those baby steps, you'll see farther, and you can start achieving larger and larger goals.

> **The most important thing about motivation is goal setting. You should always have a goal.**
>
> **—Francie Larrieu Smith, five-time U.S. Olympic Team member**

Think about this. In 2003, Annika Sorenstam was the first woman to play in a Professional Golfers' Association (PGA) tournament in fifty-eight years. Most people recognize Annika by name because of this accomplishment. But, was playing in the PGA Sorenstam's destination, her definition of success? No, it was just one of the steps along the way, one aspect of her strategy for improving her game and achieving her dreams. Her strategy worked. She elevated her game and she won two major women's golf tournaments that same year. Today Annika is arguably the most successful female golfer of all time. She has won an incredible number of tournaments and awards and has earned more than $20 million, which is more than any other Ladies Professional Golf Association (LPGA) player ever.

Goal setting is an ongoing, life-changing process that will have a profound impact on your performance. As you achieve each goal you set, you should replace it with a new one. In recrafting your strategy, you need to recognize that your mind will only accept a goal that is slightly bigger than the goal you've just achieved because it perceives it as realistic or attainable. So if your goal is to earn $1,000 a week, when you achieve this earning level, you should set your next goal to earn $1,200. Attaining these goals will give you confidence and momentum. By constantly stretching yourself you will elevate your performance and move closer to your ultimate destination, while achieving success all along the way.

YOU GOTTA CONSTANTLY REVIEW YOUR GOALS

Once you have clearly defined your goals and have a strategy for achieving them, I recommend placing them in areas where you can constantly review them. For example, if you place them by your bed, you can read them at night before you go to sleep and again in the morning when you wake up. If you want to take it a step further, put them places where you'll see them as you go about your day. I have placed my goals on the dashboard of my car, the bathroom mirror, and the top of my laptop.

> **Review your goals twice every day in order to be focused on achieving them.**
>
> **—Les Brown, motivational speaker**

You can internalize your goals by reading the words out loud and with strong emotion. The more often you read your goals to yourself, the faster your momentum will increase and the sooner you'll see results.

Why? Because input equals output. As you read each goal, visualize yourself achieving it. For instance, if your goal is to win a sales contest, mentally picture yourself walking across the stage to receive the recognition while your family and friends cheer you on. Really feel the joy and pride of accomplishment as you see yourself attain your goal.

When you consistently review and visualize your goals, they become embedded in a part of your brain called the reticular activating system (RAS). The RAS amplifies your thoughts and stimulates your ability to turn your goals into reality. It's like a filter that sifts out the things that don't pertain to your goals and brings the most important things into focus.

Here's an example of how the RAS works: Have you ever bought a car and then suddenly started seeing that kind of car everywhere? Those cars were always there, but you never noticed them because your mind filtered them out. But once you got that new car, your RAS brought into focus all the cars that look just like yours.

According to Jim Madrid of Entelechy Training and Development, the same thing happens when you write down your goals and evaluate them regularly—you

Soon your goals will become so important that physically and mentally you must achieve them.

stimulate the RAS and put it to work. Just like with the new car, your brain starts to notice anything that relates to your dreams and the goals you have set. The RAS helps you say, do, act, and react in ways that move you in the direction of your dreams and goals.

As you begin saying, doing, acting, and reacting in this new way, your goals will start to become real. You will wake up with them on your mind, go to bed thinking about them, and you will even dream about them. It's not that you've changed that much consciously, but subconscious changes are taking place.

Many times you won't even realize these changes are happening. But as you keep thinking about and internalizing your goals, you'll start to walk differently, talk differently, and think differently. Your work ethic will improve, and you will become more positive about what you're doing. You'll begin to make the right moves, and you'll start getting results.

Soon your goals will become so important that physically and mentally you must achieve them. They will become a real part of who you are, creating a burning desire inside that drives and motivates you. Most importantly, they will influence your thinking and become your guidance system for life.

Whatever goals you have set for your career, company, finances, or personal life, you won't achieve them overnight. But rest assured, once you set your goals, write them down, and commit to reviewing them every day, you will move quickly in the direction of your dreams.

As you work toward accomplishing your dreams and the goals you've set for yourself and travel this exciting road to

> **As you work toward accomplishing your dreams and the goals you've set for yourself and travel this exciting road to success, you're going to have some hiccups.**

success, you're going to have some hiccups. Some negative things will inevitably happen to you along the way. You'll have setbacks and disappointments. However, if you stay focused on your goals by constantly reviewing them, you will get back on course and keep moving down the path that will lead you to your dreams . . . the ultimate destination you desire.

YOU GOTTA HAVE A DREAM BOOK

If you really want to achieve your dreams, you need to take goal setting to the next level by using a concept known as a dream book. I originally developed the dream book as a way to help me set, manage, and achieve my own dreams and goals. You can turn your dreams into attainable goals by using the same tool.

A dream book is a notebook or scrapbook in which you write down, prioritize, and expand your dreams. It's a lot like a playbook in sports. A playbook lists all the possible plays a team could run and how to run them. It shows them in great detail, usually with diagrams and pictures. The playbook also indicates which plays to use when—for example, which plays to run on short yardage and which plays to run if you're facing third down and twenty yards.

When it's completed, your dream book should list all your dreams plus the steps you need to take to achieve them. It should show your dreams in great detail, with pictures, so that you can clearly envision them. It should also establish which goals to work on short-term and which ones to work on long-term. When you use the dream book to specifically define your goals, you'll start making progress immediately. I have never found a better way to set and achieve goals than by using the steps in the dream book.

When you use the dream book to specifically define your goals, you'll start making progress immediately.

Creating a dream book takes some time and focus, so instead of giving you the process here and now, I've provided it at the end of the book. When you are ready to sit down and commit yourself to defining and achieving your dreams, turn to that section of the book and follow the steps outlined.

For those of you who don't already have a dream book, I can't encourage you enough to get one. You simply won't believe the impact it will have on your income and success. And for those of you who already have one, when was the last time you looked at it? Perhaps it's time to update it or get a new one altogether. You'll be glad you did.

To win, you gotta have a dream.

To have a dream, you gotta

- Know where you're going
- Write down your goals
- Have a strategy
- Constantly review your goals
- Have a dream book

★ CHAPTER 3 ★

YOU GOTTA THINK LIKE A WINNER

EARLY IN MY SALES CAREER, I was invited to a training seminar several hours from home. I decided to attend and caught a ride with an associate named Ken. Ken was an experienced salesman, doing a great job and making lots of money. I was a young rookie who asked a lot of questions. I could tell Ken got tired of answering my questions, but I kept asking because I was eager to learn.

> Winners are those people who make a habit of doing the things losers are uncomfortable doing.
>
> —Ed Foreman, author and inspirational speaker

Eventually, he threw me a book and said, "Read it." I did and from that day on I became hooked on learning the strategies of success. I started reading books like *The Power of Positive Thinking* by Norman Vincent Peale and *See You at the Top* by Zig Ziglar. As I read those books, I began to understand that we become what we spend the most time thinking about. Then I remembered what the *Bible* says: "As a man thinks in his heart, so is he." This concept, that we become what we think about most often, is actually one of the foundational concepts of most self-improvement or high-performance principles.

Our thoughts determine our actions, our moods, our self-image, how we present ourselves to others, and even the words we speak. The simplest and quickest way to change our situation in life is simply to change the way we think. In short, our thoughts determine our destiny. You are today where your thoughts have brought you, and you will be tomorrow where your thoughts take you. If you want to improve your life, grow your business, and generate more sales, you gotta think like a winner.

I wanted to be a top performer, a winner, an all-star, and I realized that to be one I had to start thinking like one. Although I had achieved some success, I knew I needed to change my thinking if I was going to achieve the kind of success I really desired. So I began to diligently study success principles by reading lots of books, listening to audio programs, and attending seminars and training events led by some of the world's leading experts in success and high performance. I discovered there is one distinctive trait that all winners have: they know that success is a mental game—they understand the power of positive thinking.

If you want to win your game, you gotta think like a winner. And you must use both offensive and defensive strategies. Offensive strategies for winning include visualizing success, controlling your attitude, and expecting victory. Defense is about protecting yourself, and guarding your mind against negativity should be your number one defensive strategy.

If you want to win your game, you gotta think like a winner.

YOU GOTTA VISUALIZE SUCCESS

Almost all high-performance individuals practice the concept of visualization. Professional and Olympic athletes include visualization techniques in their practice schedules. They set their goals and then visualize themselves achieving those goals over and over again in their minds. All else being equal, these top performers know that winning is a mental issue. The better prepared they are mentally, the better they will perform when it really counts.

In the 1984 Olympics, the pressure was on Mary Lou Retton to become the first American woman to win the gold medal in the all-around individual gymnastics competition. But she needed a perfect score of 10.0 on the vault. She had visualized herself flawlessly performing her routine literally hundreds of times. When the time came to do it for real, her body was able to execute the routine perfectly, and she won the gold. What the mind can conceive and believe, the body can achieve.

> **Visualization lets you concentrate on all the positive aspects of your game.**
>
> **—Curtis Strange, PGA player and champion**

Visualization involves repeatedly imagining a scene or goal with intense clarity and feeling. It goes beyond just reading your goals and dreams to purposefully visualizing yourself achieving them. Vivid mental pictures are as real to your subconscious mind as actual experiences. Your physical body and subconscious mind can't tell the difference between something that actually happens to you and something you vividly imagine is happening to you. Psychologists have proven this by attaching electrodes to Olympic athletes and testing their mental stimulation during visualization exercises. The psychologists determined that the athletes experienced the same impulses while visualizing their routines as they did when they actually performed the routines.

That's why many of the top coaches shoot video footage of their team's plays, edit it to show only the very best plays, and then have their players review the film. Repeatedly seeing their peak performance levels sends a powerful message to the players' subconscious minds about their capabilities. The result is actual improvement in the players' performances in the game.

You can do the same thing in sales. By visualizing positive results you actually change your beliefs and develop confidence in your ability to achieve any result you desire. Belief is simply the feeling of certainty that something is going to happen. Positive belief is exactly the opposite of fear; it is faith. It is the total expectation that you will succeed.

Positive belief is exactly the opposite of fear; it is faith.

I learned years ago to use the power of visualization in my sales career, and then I started teaching others to do the same. For twelve years I managed a sales office. In ten of those years, our office was either number one or two in the nation. Our team never had fewer than five of the top twenty salespeople in the company; and three different times we had the number one salesperson in the world. The secret to our success was that each salesperson developed goals and then regularly visualized him- or herself hitting the target.

Using visualization techniques enhanced my team's beliefs, attitudes, and expectations. Visualizing their success improved my team's behavior and instantly elevated their performance. When their performance soared upward, so did their sales and our business. It is a small difference that gave them an edge.

Top-notch businesspeople routinely rehearse their presentations in their minds. Legendary motivational speaker Zig Ziglar says he usually spends two to three hours mentally preparing before he gives a speech, even though it may be one he's given many times before. His goal is to give a fantastic speech that exceeds expectations, and he knows mental

FORMULA FOR THINKING
LIKE A WINNER

If you change your thoughts . . .
>you will change your beliefs.

If you change your beliefs . . .
>you will change your expectations.

If you change your expectations . . .
>you will change your attitude.

If you change your attitude . . .
>you will change your behavior.

If you change your behavior . . .
>you will change your performance.

If you change your performance . . .
>you will change your life.

preparation—including visualizing himself performing the speech—improves his results.

The key to visualization is to not merely think about your dreams and goals, but also to see, feel, and touch them in your mind's eye. Feel the success of completing your goals with strong emotions. Find a quiet place, close your eyes, and mentally picture what you want to happen as if it were real and actually occurring in the present.

If you want to be a champion salesperson, you gotta dedicate time to mentally preparing. Always take a few minutes prior to each sales call or presentation to visualize each step of the process. If you're traveling to meet a potential client, pull over to the side of the road and relax for a few minutes. Get a clear, vivid picture in your mind of the specific outcome or results you desire from the meeting. This will help you get in the right mental state to win.

If a task or goal seems impossible to accomplish, it's because you're only using the conscious, mechanical part of your mind. Visualization taps into the subconscious part of your mind and unleashes the incredible power that comes from absolute inner certainty. Use visualization when you need to close the big sale, when you need a 10.0 to win, and when you must perform to ensure your success. Visualizing the end result will no doubt guarantee victory for you and your team.

YOU GOTTA CONTROL YOUR ATTITUDE

To think like a winner, you gotta learn to control your attitude each and every day. It all starts with you. You are the CEO of You, Incorporated. Jack Welch, the former head of General Electric, summed up the truth about attitude when he said, "Nothing of any importance has ever been accomplished by a pessimist."

> **You have to believe in yourself when no one else does—that makes you a winner.**
>
> **—Venus Williams, women's tennis champion**

Most people just don't understand that your attitude can be your best friend or your worst enemy. It can take you to levels you never thought possible, or it can be the single most limiting element in your life. Your attitude—good or bad—is contagious. It spreads to others you come in contact with— your coworkers, your family, and especially your clients. It affects everything you do.

Having a bad attitude will cost you sales, business, friends, time, and energy. You will never make it to the top of your game if you consistently have "stinkin' thinkin'." Of course, everyone has bad days and gets down once in a while. However, if you learn to control your attitude, your consistent thoughts and beliefs will always prevail.

When you have a good attitude, good things happen. The adage that success is 90 percent attitude and 10 percent aptitude is true. I've always noticed that the salespeople with the best attitudes sell more. All superstars have a super attitude. They absolutely refuse to major in the minors or let the small stuff get them down.

Having a good attitude is a deliberate, conscious choice, and making this choice starts with knowing where your attitude is every day. Consciously analyze your attitude—give yourself a mental checkup. Ask yourself, "How is my attitude today? Is it great, bad, or just okay?" If the answer is "bad" or "okay," what can you do to change your attitude? Think about what has caused your attitude to slip. Is it just the normal negatives of life or is there something unusual or major going on?

Next, determine if this is a situation you can control. If it is, take the steps necessary to get the situation back on track. Even if you can't do anything to improve the situation, you can always learn something from it and control your attitude.

Whether your attitude is great, bad, or just okay, you should work to improve it every day. If you don't reinforce a positive attitude, it will turn negative over time. Just as an athlete's muscles will become weak if he or she doesn't exercise them, your attitude will deteriorate if you neglect it. Here are some things you can do to improve your attitude:

- Read positive books.
- Listen to motivational audio programs.
- Visualize your goals and future successes constantly.
- Associate with positive people.
- View every negative situation as a challenge or an opportunity for improvement.

Having a good attitude is a deliberate, conscious choice, and making this choice starts with knowing where your attitude is every day.

YOU GOTTA EXPECT VICTORY

Do you wake up in the morning thinking, "This is going to be a lousy day" or "Nothing good ever happens to me"? If you have an important presentation to make, do you tell yourself, "I don't have a chance at closing this sale"? If you routinely think this way, how does your day turn out? Do you make the sale? I'd be willing to bet you get exactly the results you expected.

> **I've always made a total effort, even when the odds seemed entirely against me. I never quit trying; I never felt that I didn't have a chance to win.**
>
> **—Arnold Palmer, PGA legend and Hall of Famer**

Winners wake up every morning with excitement, enthusiasm, and confidence, knowing that success is in store for them. Top performers set their minds for victory; they set their minds for success.

Setting your mind for success doesn't happen automatically. You have to constantly tell yourself "today is a great day, good things are happening, and new and exciting doors are opening." Go out each and every day believing success will come your way.

Now, you may think, "My business isn't doing well, nobody will buy from me, and I can't pay my bills. How can I live with enthusiasm? How can I be positive when I have so many problems?"

If you will consistently think about and focus on what you want, you will ultimately get it.

You gotta make a decision that you're going to have confident expectancy about everything you do. You have to continually expect that things are going to get better. Positive expectation is a conscious choice and a habit of faith. It is a conscious choice to see a positive outcome instead of a negative one. As you think, so it is created. As you believe, so it is done.

Expectancy is about seeing beyond where you are. Look out into the future and see yourself as successful, happy, and enthusiastic. See sales coming your way, see yourself having all the contacts you want and watch your income soar. See things better than they are . . . see them as you want them to be. Develop a habit of focusing on what's right in your world instead of what's wrong, on what you have instead of what you don't have, on your talents instead of on your weaknesses.

You're probably asking, "What if I do that and it doesn't work?"

My question to you is, "What if you do it and it *does* work?"

If you will consistently think about and focus on what you want, you will ultimately get it. By focusing on positive thoughts, you open up your mind to start attracting success. This is why top salespeople seem to effortlessly sell so much more than average negative-thinking salespeople. People want to do business with positive, upbeat, successful individuals.

When things look impossible or you're tempted to go through the day negative and self-destructive, that is when you have to step up and change your belief level. Expect good things to happen. Expect to rise above your challenges. Expect victory!

When those around you predict doom and gloom for everything from the economy to your dreams and goals, remember that success in life, business, and sales is mostly a mental game. Your thoughts will drive your results, your success, even your destiny. So proactively focus on the positive, defend your mind against the negative, and expect victory. You have the power to choose your thoughts and your attitude and, therefore, your success.

YOU GOTTA GUARD YOUR MIND

You can give 100 percent day and night and you can use all the offensive strategies in your playbook, but unless you guard your mind, it's unlikely you will live up to your full potential. That's because there is a constant battle going on in your mind between positive and negative thoughts. Remember, you will become what you think about most of the time. If you make the mistake of dwelling on negative thoughts, you're going to end up being someone and somewhere you don't want to be. Negative thinking will destroy your dreams and wreck everything you have achieved through hard work.

In our society, too many people are mentally out of shape. Most people have never learned how to control their

**Remember, you will become
what you think about most of
the time.**

thoughts. As a result, they don't have the desire or the strength to choose positive thoughts and eliminate or replace negative ones. When our mental muscles are weak, we are easily swayed by the influences, opinions, and ideas of others.

There are two main sources of negativity that continually assault our minds and thoughts:

Our environment Outside influences feed us negative information virtually all day long. Did you know Americans watch an average of seven hours of TV a day? And if we're not in front of the TV, we're probably reading the newspaper, listening to the radio, or checking the latest gossip magazines. Consider this: News has to sell. What sells better—positive or negative news?

Unfortunately, most of us are also surrounded by pessimistic people—business associates, peers, family members, even people we casually come in contact with. Most of these people aren't intentionally negative; they're just affected by the same pessimistic environment we are. However, that doesn't change the fact that if we constantly listen to negative, defeatist people, we will become negative and defeatist ourselves.

Self-destructive thoughts Too many people believe that their past equals their future. In other words, they think that their past failures and disappointments will continue and that they'll never achieve the success they desire. Much of our negative self-talk comes from bad experiences or bad feedback we've had: clients rejected us, bosses chastised us, family members berated us. If we allow ourselves to continue this harmful self-talk, our thinking becomes a self-fulfilling prophecy. If we think thoughts of defeat and mediocrity, we will live a defeated life.

Most people aren't aware of how negative their thinking really is and how many of their thoughts are self-destructive. Try this quick exercise: For just one hour, jot down every thought that pops into your head, every comment you make to yourself, and every judgment you make about yourself. At the end of the hour, tally up how many are negative and how many are positive. Unless you have already learned how to guard your mind and focus on the good, I can virtually guarantee that the self-destructive thoughts will far outnumber the encouraging ones.

To guard against all this negativity, you gotta get in shape mentally. If you don't defend yourself against negative influences, you'll wind up drained and sitting on the sidelines. You must train your mind and develop the mental muscle and the will to resist the negativity that comes at you from all directions. Condition yourself to think positively, or you'll go back to the pessimistic state of mind most people live in. If you don't control your mind, it will control you.

> **Positive thinking is the key to success in business, education, pro football, anything that you can mention. I go out there thinking that I'm going to complete every pass.**
>
> **—Ron Jaworski, National Football League Hall of Famer**

Here are just a few steps you can take to guard your mind:

1. **See things as they really are.** Do a mental checkup to make sure you have a true and clear picture of reality. It's easy to lull yourself into thinking that your situation is worse than the truth. Ninety-five percent of what we worry about never happens, and the five percent that does happen is never quite as bad as we imagined. When you consistently take a negative view of situations you become overwhelmed and discouraged.

2. **Be aware of your thoughts.** Are they positive and uplifting or negative and destructive? Consistently ask yourself, "Is this the type of thinking that empowers me and builds me up, or discourages me and makes me weak?" Self-awareness is the first step to making a change.

3. **Get rid of any negative thoughts immediately.** It only takes a little bit of poison to kill success. Cancel negative thoughts by saying the words, "Cancel, cancel."

4. **Replace negative thoughts with positive ones.** Keep your mind strong by feeding it positive thoughts of success. Anyone can find problems. If you want to be a top

performer, choose to find the positive in every situation. You'll find it if you look hard enough.

If you practice these skills every day, eventually they will become habits, and you will exponentially change your ability to sell more and achieve all-star success.

To win, you gotta think like a winner.

To think like a winner, you gotta

- Visualize success
- Control your attitude
- Expect victory
- Guard your mind

★ CHAPTER 4 ★

YOU GOTTA GET THE COMPETITIVE ADVANTAGE

IF WE'RE TOTALLY HONEST about it, most of us dreamed of being stars when we were young. We dreamed of making the winning shot, catching the Hail Mary pass, receiving the perfect score from the judges, or winning the Miss America pageant. Most kids on the playground dream of winning a championship game or a gold medal. Even kids who don't like sports still want to compete and win in music, the arts, the classroom, or some other pursuit.

From early childhood, competition plays an important role in our lives. You see, competition is what makes us better. It awakens the mind and activates the body, quickens the pulse and heightens awareness. When you compete, everything else fades into the background and you become more focused. In the midst of competition, time seems to suspend itself—you are unaware of just how long you've played the game. And you begin to really care about the outcome—you want to win.

> A competitor will find a way to win. Competitors take bad breaks and use them to drive themselves just that much harder. Quitters take bad breaks and use them as reasons to give up.
>
> —Nancy Lopez, LPGA Hall of Famer

You can win some games just by competing in the moment. But to consistently win long-term and become an all-star, you gotta create and maintain a competitive advantage. This distinct advantage is what allows you to consistently outperform the competition and put together a lasting winning streak.

Some people have convinced themselves that to get a competitive advantage means disregarding the rules or cheating in some way. Nothing could be further from the truth. To gain an advantage takes hard work—you must excel at everything to move past your competition. You must challenge yourself and believe in yourself, and you gotta want to win.

YOU GOTTA LOVE A GOOD CHALLENGE

To gain the competitive advantage, you gotta love a good challenge. Mountain climbers aren't fascinated by molehills. They want the challenge of a harsh climate and thin air, of seemingly impossible heights. They accept that rocks fall, ropes fray, and muscles become weak and exhausted. That's what they love about it. They are eager to prove to themselves that they have what it takes to conquer the challenges and reach the top.

> **To succeed, you need to find something
> to hold on to, something to motivate you,
> something to inspire you.**
>
> **—Tony Dorsett, NFL Hall of Famer**

The same is true of top salespeople—they love a challenge. They're not interested in easy-to-achieve targets or quotas. They want goals that will make them stretch and grow; they want to be number one. They know some people won't buy and some customers will cancel sales along the way, but that doesn't deter them. They want to find out if they have what it takes to be the very best, no matter what challenges or unforeseen difficulties they might encounter.

The thing that is often so unsatisfying about our careers (and many times, our lives) is not that the success we desire is too hard to attain. In fact, it's the opposite. It's that we have lowered the standards that define success, and we expect success to be easy and predictable. As a result, we feel unchallenged and rather empty.

But when we seek challenges—take on new responsibilities, tackle the projects and tasks that no one else will—we start to rise above the crowd and climb ever higher into the thin air of real success. We need to realize that it is the biggest challenges that are worthy of our best efforts.

YOU GOTTA CREATE A BURNING DESIRE

Athletes and teams don't win championships unless each individual wants to win so fiercely that he or she would do just about anything to make it happen. The same is true for each of us—if we're going to win our "championship," we have to commit ourselves to do whatever it takes to ensure victory. We must find and nurture that burning desire to win.

We must find and nurture that burning desire to win.

Deep inside of most of us, there is a desire to win. Unfortunately, many people lose that desire somewhere along the way. Maybe they've faced so many failures they've convinced themselves they will never win. Or perhaps they just don't have enough reasons to motivate themselves. The more reasons you have to achieve something, the more desire, inspiration, and motivation will exist inside of you.

I've never played a game that I didn't want to win. It is this intrinsic desire for competing and winning that attracted me to sales. And yet, there's a big difference between just wanting to win and having a burning desire to win. I know, because I didn't always have a burning desire to rise to the top of my profession. And let me tell you, it makes all the difference in the world.

> **The difference between the impossible and the possible lies in a person's determination.**
>
> —Tommy Lasorda, professional baseball hall of famer

Do you remember the story about my car being repossessed? Well, just a few weeks after that, I had the opportunity to attend our company's national sales convention with my wife. However, at this point in my career, I was at the bottom, couldn't afford to go, and didn't understand the value of attending meetings and training events. So we missed the first day and didn't think anything of it.

I will never know exactly why, but the second day, I woke up before dawn and decided we were going to that meeting. Susan thought I was crazy because the meeting was a four-hour drive away, and we wouldn't arrive until noon. But it didn't matter; I knew we had to go.

Although we were only there for the second half of the second day, attending this meeting had a profound impact on my life. There were featured speakers and top achievers from across the nation. I don't remember who the presenters were, but I will never forget one statement made by one of the top money earners in the country: "Set yourself on fire, and people will gather to watch you burn." I didn't really understand what he meant, but it was a catchy phrase that stuck in my mind.

Later that evening, we attended the awards banquet where the top producers received bonuses and recognition for a job well done. What I especially noticed was the excitement, emotion, attitude, and pride the winners had about their successes. Their actions and the atmosphere at the event reminded me of something you would experience at an Olympic awards ceremony. These high-performance individuals had that "in the gut" burning desire to win. I realized this was the same drive that star athletes (or anyone else who achieves incredible success) must have to make it to the very top of their games. It was then I understood that these top performers were "on fire." They absolutely radiated success, motivation, and passion. It didn't matter if they were eighteen or eighty; they had a burning desire to win, and people gathered to watch the glow.

> **Winning isn't everything, but wanting to win is.**
>
> **—Vince Lombardi, legendary NFL coach and Hall of Famer**

Although I had felt this burning desire to win in sports, I had never experienced it with my sales career. I realized that if I was going to achieve my full potential, I had to find a way to dig deep inside and ignite this passion. And that's what I did!

As Susan and I drove home from the convention that night, all I could think about was how I could take my struggling team to the top. Everything else seemed to fade into the darkness of the winding road. As we approached a small town, a bright neon sign in front of a bank startled me. In big bold letters that seemed to shout out at me, the sign said: SUCCESS BEGINS WITH CAN. FAILURE BEGINS WITH CAN'T.

The key is to focus on the one thing you want so desperately that you will move heaven and earth to get it.

I decided then and there that I would never again settle for less than my very best, that I would eliminate the word "can't" from my thinking and vocabulary. I was going to set myself on fire through my attitudes and actions. I also decided that I would build one of the top sales teams in the nation and that I would give a speech at next year's convention. I was so convinced that I started writing the speech that night.

From that point on, my team started to believe we could win, and we became competitive. We were glowing with enthusiasm and positive expectancy. We worked hard that year and our sales grew at record pace. At the next convention, our company rewarded my team for their exceptional efforts and we celebrated our success together. I was also asked to give a speech, and as you might have guessed, I gave the speech I had started the year before in the middle of the night. The first words I said were, "Success begins with can. Failure begins with can't." What a difference a year can make if you just decide to get in the game and believe you can win.

I also learned the power of the words "can" and "can't." Now I know whichever word you use consistently becomes a self-fulfilling prophecy.

Throughout the years, I've worked with thousands of people from every walk of life, and one of the questions I am asked on a consistent basis is, "How do I get this burning desire to win?"

The key is to focus on the one thing you want so desperately that you will move heaven and earth to get it. I discovered that when you want something—I mean really, really want it—there is a reaction that goes off inside you that says, "YES!" The energy that is released in that moment of desire creates one of the most powerful and magnetic forces in the universe.

So, ask yourself, "Of all my dreams and goals, which one is the most important . . . what do I want more than anything in the world?" Stop right now and jot down your answer.

Next, write down all of the reasons why achieving this goal is a must. The whys will wake you up early and keep you up late. The whys will give you purpose, passion, and power. When you know the reasons why you work you will get a burning desire that will propel you to go the extra mile. Now, mentally link achieving the goal to your career. Make your products and services your tool, your method, to achieving your heart's desires. This will motivate you to take the necessary actions to increase your performance to all-star levels. If you have the need, you will create the burning desire to make it happen.

YOU GOTTA GET THE MENTAL EDGE

I know a lot of salespeople with average talents and abilities who are multimillionaires. I also know a lot of very talented salespeople who are broke and in debt. What's the difference? The multimillionaires understand the importance of having a mental edge.

> **Change your thoughts and you can change your world.**
>
> **—Dr. Norman Vincent Peale, author of the great inspirational, best-selling book of all time, *The Power of Positive Thinking***

How well you perform involves much more than the sum of your talents, skills, abilities, and experience. Strong mental preparation is often the difference between the winners and the also-rans. Elite athletes know the truth behind the adage "Winning is 90 percent mental and 10 percent physical." In fact, many of them believe that having a mental edge is so important that they hire sports psychologists or performance experts to help them get it and keep it.

If you want to perform at an elite level, you gotta learn how to develop a mental edge. Then you must do what it takes to stay in top mental shape. Developing your mind is a lot like developing your body. First, you have to identify the areas you want to improve, like getting rid of a fat belly and love handles, or toning your arms and shoulders. Then you have to establish and follow a training regimen to eliminate the flab and strengthen and build the muscles. You can get your mind in shape by following the same steps. So let's get started.

Step 1: Identify Areas to Improve

Well begun is half done. Doctors say accurate diagnosis is half the cure, so if you really want to change you gotta identify the areas you need to improve. Let's start with your mental problem areas—the mind games that hold you back and keep

Developing your mind is a lot like developing your body.

you from performing at your peak ability. Some examples are fears, limiting or false beliefs, doubts about yourself and your abilities, and destructive self-talk. Perhaps you have a negative attitude about something or someone on your team. Maybe you're overwhelmed by the fear of giving a presentation or asking a customer for the order. Or perhaps you lack motivation and discipline. If you can identify and eliminate these problem areas, you will gain the critical mental edge.

Write down all the areas you can think of that need improvement. From this list, pick the three that represent your biggest obstacles to success.

Now let's look at your existing strengths. These are qualities, characteristics, behaviors, and actions that contribute to your success. Write down all of your strengths. We all have strengths—plenty of them—and there's tremendous value in knowing what they are.

From your list of strengths, pick the three that, if you improved them to the next level, would have the biggest impact on your success.

Step 2: Establish a Training Regimen

Creating and reading affirmations eliminates your problem areas and strengthens your strengths. An affirmation is a positive statement about you. It describes specific traits or characteristics you want to develop or the type of person you want to be. Effective affirmations are stated

- With action-oriented phrases that begin with the words "because" or "by"
- In the first person, using the words "I" and "my"
- In the present tense, using the word "am" instead of "will be"
- In the positive, without using words such as "not" or "don't"
- In concise and clear terms—they are short and specific

These phrases describe the actions you know you must take to make change possible.

For each of the three problem areas you identified, you're going to develop a positive affirmation. For example, an affirmation for a basketball player struggling with free throws could be, "Because of my perfect form and spectacular shooting skills, I am a consistent 70 percent free-throw shooter." If your problem area is really big, your affirmation should represent a small step toward eliminating it.

Here are some examples of common problem areas and affirmations for salespeople:

- Fear of contacting prospects: "Because I work my leads as if they are gold, I have more than enough prospects to see each and every day."

- Poor work habits: "Because I understand the importance of hard work and discipline, I am a self-motivated person who has an excellent work ethic."
- Problems with presenting and closing: "Because of my strong ability to present and close, I consistently close over 70 percent of the prospects I see."

Write down an affirmation for each of your own problem areas. Then, completely erase or mark through the problem so that you can't read it anymore. This is the first step in getting rid of your old negative habits.

Now go back and develop a positive affirmation that will enhance each of your three strengths. Below are some examples of strengthening affirmations:

- Because I am committed to studying the latest strategies and techniques, I am constantly improving my communication skills.
- I raise the bar daily in all areas of my performance in sales and marketing by staying focused and committed to my dreams and goals.
- I am an exceptionally talented manager who demands more of myself than others expect of me.
- I stay ahead of the competition by making my good better and my better best.

Step 3: Follow the Training Regimen

With any fitness plan, if you don't follow it, you won't see any changes. The same is true of your mental fitness plan. You gotta follow the plan and exercise your mind every single day. Read all your affirmations daily along with your goals, especially in the morning (when you awaken or on your way to work) and in the evening before going to sleep.

For the best results, read them out loud and with commitment and emotion. Speaking your affirmations is more than a mental workout; it's also an emotional workout. It sends a message to your brain that you mean it. When you positively affirm something with emotion on a consistent basis, you stimulate the RAS in your brain to open up your mind to the possibilities of your success. You truly can speak things into existence.

At this point you're probably saying, "Billy, you're crazy. You're telling me to talk to myself out loud? People are going to think I'm nuts!" My response is, "Aren't your dreams and goals worth feeling a little nuts?" I hope your answer is yes. But the good news is you can actually make it fun. With modern technology, people will simply think you're talking on your cell phone hands-free, especially if you say your affirmations in the car. Just look over, smile, and keep affirming!

I've never known anyone who consistently spoke his or her affirmations out loud, engaging the body and emotions with total belief, who did not have a total transformation. I promise that you will see a dramatic impact on your performance if all you do is speak your affirmations for five minutes each day before work. It will make a noticeable impact in your attitude, your thinking, and how people respond to you each day.

By reciting your affirmations daily, you will develop a mental edge by overcoming your problem areas and elevating your strengths. And, as with exercise, the more you affirm your desires, the faster you'll see results. It's all about repetition and consistency.

Follow these simple steps, and you will develop the mental edge that will take you to the top of your game.

YOU GOTTA MAKE IT A GAME

If you're playing to win, you gotta make whatever you're doing a game. Games promote competition, and competition challenges you to rise to levels you have never reached before.

> **I play to win, whether during practice or a real game. And I will not let anything get in the way of my competitive enthusiasm to win.**
>
> **—Michael Jordan, NBA Hall of Famer**

Imagine that you're at a football game. Just before the running back is about to cross the goal line for a touchdown, he stops running, lays the ball on the ground, and walks off the field. Now, that would never happen. Maybe it would during practice, but the fact that it's a game makes us want to beat the competition. It makes us care more about winning.

It's relatively easy to make sales a game because most sales organizations inherently understand the power of the game concept. That is why they create contests, bonuses, and awards. I've always noticed that, in sales, the people who work to win the contests and achieve the awards always make the money. Why? Because of the competition. Most people will work harder for awards and recognition than for money because of the satisfaction they get from beating the competition and winning the game. Every salesperson who has ever told me the awards and recognition didn't mean anything was not being honest with himself.

To really make sales a game for our organization, we created an atmosphere where people felt like they were part of a team, where they were given the opportunity to win, and that made them want to compete. To accomplish this, we simply incorporated a few of the elements that exist within a game or contest. For example, we "kept score" by tracking everyone's progress and constantly updating our "scoreboard" so that everyone could see who was winning the game.

Having a scoreboard is an essential element of any game. Constantly showing the score helps you know where you are, evaluate your performance, and make the adjustments necessary to win. In our organization, the scoreboard was a marker board and some simple charts and graphs that showed key information for every salesperson, including sales goals, the number of prospects seen, and closing ratio. Everyone could compare themselves to other salespeople, and as a team, we were able to determine whether we were winning. We challenged our salespeople to set goals, to compete with each other, and to outperform the competition.

Constantly showing the score helps you know where you are, evaluate your performance, and make the adjustments necessary to win.

I've used this same type of scoring system to help organizations and individuals increase their performance and achieve record results. Regardless of your career or endeavor, you can incorporate elements of a game to encourage healthy competition. You can create a competitive environment in virtually any profession and provide a reward for almost every situation. (For example, if you accomplish a personal goal, you can reward yourself by buying something you've always wanted or celebrate with your spouse or significant other at a special restaurant.) I encourage you to develop a scoreboard. All you have to do is determine the top three or four criteria for success for your particular endeavor and then track your results for those criteria.

> **You can create a competitive environment in virtually any profession and provide a reward for almost every situation.**

When everyone competes, everyone wins. The company wins because it increases productivity, results, and profits. The top performer wins and receives the awards and recognition he or she desires. Even those individuals who don't achieve top honors win because they almost always achieve more than they would have if they hadn't competed.

Competition encourages us to do our best, and ultimately, that is what determines the real winners. If you know in your heart that you've given your all and put forth your best effort, then you'll always win no matter what the scoreboard says.

Decide to be a competitor. Leave it all on the playing field. Always accept the biggest challenges and give them your best efforts. Dig deep inside and rekindle your burning desire to win. Pick out other individuals who are doing more than you and make it your goal to be better than them at the game. But most of all, compete with yourself. Every day, commit to being better than you were the day before. That's how you get the competitive advantage that will take you to the top.

To win, you gotta get the competitive advantage.

To get the competitive advantage, you gotta

- Love a good challenge
- Create a burning desire
- Get the mental edge
- Make it a game

★ CHAPTER 5 ★

YOU GOTTA PLAY
THE NUMBERS

THE POWER OF NUMBERS is the basic philosophy of the most successful businesses. Sam Walton, founder and former chairman of Wal-Mart, built his empire on the power of numbers—he developed a profitable working model and then duplicated that model over and over again. He knew that more stores meant more sales, more sales meant more profit, more profit meant more capital to build more stores, and the cycle continued. Today, Wal-Mart is the world's largest retailer.

Athletes have learned to use the power of numbers to their advantage too. The star athlete is not always the one with the most talent, but many times he will score the most points—usually because he takes the most shots. The top athletes know that winning is a numbers game—the more shots you take, the more opportunities you have to score.

> **You miss 100 percent of the shots you never take.**
>
> **—Wayne Gretzky, National Hockey League Hall of Famer**

Interestingly, the person who makes the most shots is almost always the person who misses the most. In 1927, Babe Ruth set the single-season home run record with 60 home runs. That same year, he also led the league in strikeouts with 189. Likewise, Cy Young won more games in his pitching career (511) than anyone else in the history of baseball. He also lost more games (316) than anyone has ever lost. And yet, people remember both men for their "winning" records.

I would rather have an average salesperson who is willing to "play the numbers" than a salesperson with a great closing average who takes very few shots. The salesperson that plays the numbers will always have more opportunities to close more sales.

If you want to win, you gotta play the numbers. Fortunately, you can learn how to leverage the power of numbers in everything you do. The key is to find a basic pattern or model that is simple, proven, and reproducible. Many businesses already have successful models, so you may not even have to figure out for yourself what works and what doesn't in your sales game. And many personal goals you might want to achieve—such as losing weight, getting in shape, earning a degree, or paying off debt—also have proven success patterns. All you have to do is discover and learn the success model for whatever it is you want to achieve and then repeat it on a mass scale to achieve predictable results.

YOU GOTTA LEARN AND PRACTICE THE BASICS

To use the power of numbers, you'gotta start by learning the basics—the skills and knowledge that are critical to your success. Then you gotta practice them over and over and over again until they become a habit. The better you are at the basics, the better your averages, and the better your averages, the better your chances of winning. Many Olympic champions train at least eight hours a day, six or seven days a week. They practice the basics repeatedly, day in and day out, and that's what makes them champions.

When Michael Jordan was in the tenth grade, he was cut from his high school varsity basketball team. The next morning, he got up and started practicing. He practiced constantly. He shot thousands and thousands of baskets. Sometimes he made it and sometimes he missed; but he kept shooting because he had a burning desire to get back on that team.

The next season, he made varsity and led the team to the state championship. After high school, he played at the University of North Carolina, and as a freshman, scored the game-winning shot for the national championship. Michael went on to make many more game-winning shots and eventually won six NBA championships. It's not surprising that he

The better you are at the basics, the better your averages, and the better your averages, the better your chances of winning.

also made the shot that won his final championship. Clearly, Michael could make the shot when it counted the most. He always went back to the basics and made the same shot he had made in practice thousands of times before.

You can apply the same principles outside of sports. When I got into sales, I had minimal knowledge and lacked confidence. But because of my competitive nature, I wanted to compete with the better, more experienced salespeople—the all-stars of the company. I quickly realized that if I wanted to improve my numbers, to get better, I needed to learn and practice the basics.

> **Success is nothing more than a few simple disciplines, practiced every day.**
>
> **—Jim Rohn, author and legendary motivational speaker**

In sales, the basics consist of prospecting, presenting, listening, asking the right questions, and closing. You have to practice these skills constantly. And no matter how long you've been in sales, you need to keep looking for ways to improve upon the basics.

One way to improve your basic skills is to find out what actions the highest achievers in your field perform and how they go about doing business, and then mimic their techniques. In psychology, this is called "modeling": if you replicate the same actions as successful people, in the same manner, with the same attitude, beliefs, and emotion, you will get the same results.

Once you've learned the basics, you need to get good at executing them.

I didn't understand that modeling was such a powerful concept early in my life, but I was using it, and I still consistently use it to find ways to improve. I learned the basics of sales and public speaking by watching videos and listening to audio programs of the top salespeople and the most sought-after speakers. I practiced my presentations in front of a mirror with the same tone, gestures, and intensity as these individuals. I videotaped myself to determine which areas needed to improve, and then I practiced those skills and techniques often.

Make a habit of reading the books, listening to the programs, attending the meetings, and networking with the successful individuals in your area of interest. Once you've learned the basics, you need to get good at executing them. The only way to do that is—you guessed it—practice! Then practice some more! Eventually, you will master the techniques, and they will become a natural part of your persona.

Even the most successful individuals can improve their performance if they get better at the basics. Tiger Woods has been hitting golf balls since he was a toddler, and practicing the basics remains a crucial part of his daily routine. The will to win is the will to prepare and practice, practice, practice.

YOU GOTTA USE THE POWER OF NUMBERS

In sales, it's vital that you know your averages and use them to achieve results. One of the amazing things about statistics is that measuring a single, one-time performance is relatively meaningless, but when multiple performances over time are measured, the numbers are extremely reliable. So once you understand how the law of averages works, you can use it to generate predictable results simply by playing the numbers.

Here's an example of how it works: If you are a salesperson, and on average, for every twenty people you contact, five buy, then your closing ratio is 25 percent. Once you know your average, it's easy to determine the results you need to achieve a certain goal. If your goal is to sell your product or service to fifty potential customers, you know you need to give two hundred sales presentations. It is true that you will never know which five out of twenty people will buy; but if you understand the law of averages, you don't give up if the first five don't buy or even the first fifteen don't buy!

Salespeople often ask me how they can increase their income. I explain to them that the fastest way to achieve this goal is to spend time selling to an increased number of qualified prospects. Even if your knowledge, skills, and

Once you know your average, it's easy to determine the results you need to achieve a certain goal.

averages stay the same, if you double the number of qualified prospects, you will double your sales income.

The real power of these principles happens when you combine the law of averages with massive numbers. I learned that early in my sales career. I understood that as long as I had a decent closing percentage, I didn't have to be the best in any particular area in order to be number one. All I had to do was know my averages, set a goal, and then play the numbers. I've used these same principles throughout my career for recruiting, training, and managing my businesses and their profits.

What's truly great about knowing your averages and playing the numbers is that even if you're inexperienced or have less-developed skills than the rest of the team, you can still generate just as much or more in sales than the all-stars who may have better averages than you. For instance, a salesperson who closes five sales for every twenty presentations given (a 25 percent closing ratio) can sell just as much as a person who closes five out of ten (a 50 percent closing ratio). All the person with a 5/20 average has to do is contact twenty people for every ten the 5/10 salesperson contacts. Of course, the salesperson with the 5/20 average has to give more presentations—that's why it's a numbers game.

Understanding these principles gives you confidence and power. If you're in a slump, you can always get out of it quickly by knowing your averages and playing the numbers.

YOU GOTTA EVALUATE YOUR PERFORMANCE TO IMPROVE YOUR AVERAGES

A professional baseball player always knows his averages because the difference between batting .250 and .300 can mean millions of dollars each year. Can you imagine making that kind of money for simply improving your skills just 5 percent? A few percentage points can mean the difference between being average and being an all-star, between sitting on the bench in the minor leagues and starting in the major leagues.

In May 2003 Tiger Woods was ranked first in the world through seven tournaments. His average number of strokes per tournament was 68.44. At the same time, David Frost was ranked 128th in the world through nine events. His average number of strokes per tournament was 71.83. The difference between Tiger and David was only 3.39 strokes per tournament, which is only a 5 percent difference. However, Tiger Woods's earnings were $3,287,250 and David Frost's earnings were $242,145. With a 5 percent better stroke average, Tiger Woods earned more than ten times the amount David Frost earned.

It's the same in business and in everyday life. I like to say, "The weight of a rose petal often determines which way a decision goes." In other words, the small things can make huge differences. Improving your averages by even a small percentage can mean the difference between just getting by and getting rich.

Think about it. Suppose you're in sales and your closing average is 5 out of 10, and you contact just ten people each week. If you improved your average to 6 out of 10—close just one more sale each week—you would make 52 more sales every year. If you multiply 52 by your average commission per sale, you can see the tremendous impact of improving your average! If your business had ten salespeople and all of them improved their averages by just one sale per week, your company would experience 520 more sales per year. Do you see the advantage?

Improving your averages really means improving your performance. You can improve any average or result by constantly evaluating your performance and making adjustments. Start by asking yourself these simple questions:

1. What are some areas I want to improve?
2. Which improvements would have the biggest impact on my career?
3. What are some simple steps I can take daily to become better in these areas?

When it's all said and done, one of the very best ways to improve your performance is to get more experience; and nothing gives you more experience and confidence than actual game time. If you're in sales, game time is the time you spend in front of qualified prospects. The more experience you acquire, the more skillful you become. You just gotta get in the game and take a whole lot of shots. When you miss, make some adjustments and then take some more shots. Remember: a missed shot is not a failure; it's an opportunity to move one step closer to perfecting your shot.

YOU GOTTA BE CONSISTENT

To achieve long-term success, you gotta consistently play the numbers in all areas of your life. If you're only nice to others occasionally, it's unlikely that you will have many friends or influence many people. If you only contact new prospects once or twice a month, you're never going to achieve top performer status.

Walt Disney was told no by virtually every person he talked to. They said his idea of a cartoon about a mouse was absolutely ridiculous. As a matter of fact, he was turned down by 302 bankers before he found someone who would fund his vision. Stop and just imagine the loss that millions of children and adults around the world would have experienced if Walt

Disney had not believed in his dream enough to keep playing the numbers.

You will never achieve anything of great significance if you're not willing to consistently play the numbers—and do what it takes to make sure that your numbers stay consistent. The *Bible* says, "Ask and it shall be given to you." But it goes a bit further by saying, "Seek and ye shall find" and "Knock and it shall be opened unto you." This is a powerful principle for success in anything you do. Think about it: If you consistently ask enough people, if you are constantly seeking out new opportunities, and if you are willing to knock on enough doors, then eventually doors will open, you will find the right opportunities, and you will achieve the results you desire.

Remember, winning is a numbers game, thus you gotta practice the basics, improve the averages, and consistently increase the numbers.

To win, you gotta play the numbers.

To play the numbers, you gotta

- Learn and practice the basics
- Use the power of numbers
- Evaluate your performance to improve your averages
- Be consistent

To achieve long-term success, you gotta consistently play the numbers in all areas of your life.

★ CHAPTER 6 ★

YOU GOTTA RAISE THE BAR

I'VE SPENT MY ENTIRE CAREER raising my personal bar higher and higher. It began with learning how to sell, then becoming a top salesperson, and then recruiting and managing people. With each step came the opportunity to challenge myself and stretch my comfort zone.

> **Nobody's a natural. You work hard to get good and then work to get better.**
>
> **—Paul Coffey, Canadian hockey hall of fame inductee**

You can't focus on being a winner without focusing on what it's going to take to get you there.

There is an old saying that states, "By the mile it's a trial; by the yard it's hard; but by the inch it's a cinch." You can raise your bar by taking one small step at a time. Every time you succeed, consider what it took to get there. Evaluate what worked and what didn't. Then you gotta raise the bar again by setting a new, bigger goal. Once you raise the bar to new heights, it's unlikely your performance will fall to its former level.

John Wooden, former coach of the UCLA Bruins, probably represents the greatest level of consistent success in sports history. He created a dynasty beyond description. In his last years with the Bruins, Coach Wooden won ten of twelve NCAA championships, seven of them consecutively. There are only four teams since 1939 that have won two in a row. Under Wooden, the Bruins won eighty-eight games in a row, had four seasons in which they didn't lose a game, and had three seasons in which they lost only one game. How did Wooden coach his team to this level of consistent success? He lived by the philosophy of constant, continuous improvement. The man with the most wins in college basketball history never talked about winning to his players: he talked to them about improving their performance every day.

Every day each player had to make some minor improvement in what he was doing. Wooden kept a journal and tracked the improvement of each player at every practice and every game. He knew that the key to success was gradual, consistent improvement.

You can't focus on being a winner without focusing on what it's going to take to get you there. It doesn't take huge leaps of improvement, only small incremental steps every day. All those incremental improvements come together and accumulate to create momentum in your life so you can experience true success.

YOU GOTTA GO THE EXTRA MILE

Part of raising the bar is going the extra mile—giving a little more, doing better than your competitors, doing better than your best. Many people say, "I can't give any more than I'm already giving" or "That's the best I can do." I say they're wrong.

In his book, *Leading from the Lockers*, John Maxwell shares the story of the first man to run a mile in under four minutes. For years, athletes had tried to break this seemingly unbreakable time barrier; experts said the human heart would explode under the conditions necessary to run a sub-four-minute mile. However, on May 6, 1954, Roger Bannister did it. He ran a mile in 3 minutes, 59 seconds.

Two amazing aspects arise from this story. The first is that Roger Bannister wasn't a professional runner. In fact, he was a medical student who set aside only forty-five minutes a day to train. But he refused to believe that he couldn't achieve this seemingly impossible goal. In his mind, he had no limits. When asked how he did it, his reply was simple and profound: "It's the ability to take more out of yourself than you've got."

> **The man who can drive himself further once the effort gets painful is the man who will win. The principle is competing against yourself. It's about self-improvement, about being better than you were the day before.**
>
> **—Steve Young, NFL Hall of Fame quarterback**

The other fascinating feature about this story is that by setting a new world record, Roger Bannister changed the sport of running forever. Within two months of Roger's achievement, John Landy set a new sub-four-minute-mile record. The next year, thirty-seven other runners broke the four-minute mile. Since Roger Bannister first set the record in 1954, hundreds of runners have run a mile in under four minutes.

So what happened? There were no great breakthroughs in training; no one discovered how to control wind resistance; human bone structure and lung power didn't suddenly improve. What happened was that someone—someone not that different from you and me—made a decision to give just a little more than he thought he had. Someone decided that he could do better than his best. Once he proved it could be done, he raised the bar for everyone else.

Never accept the idea that there's a limit to how far you can go. It's your responsibility to shatter this type of thinking, explore the realm of the untested, and discover breakthrough opportunities. Independent scholar and futurist Joel Barker, known around the world as the "Paradigm Man" for popularizing the concept of paradigm shifts, once said, "Those who say it can't be done are usually interrupted by others doing it."

The key is to commit yourself to excellence in everything you do. There's a famous saying that is on a picture I bought from Successories: "Excellence is the result of caring more than others think is wise, risking more than others think is safe, dreaming more than others think is practical, and expecting more than others think is possible." Excellence means to consistently excel, to seek constant improvement. Only then are we living a life in which we can achieve all-star status. So let me ask you a question. Are you constantly increasing the quality of your performance, the level of your dedication? Are you doing it once in awhile or are you doing it constantly, consistently? Are you going the extra mile to achieve excellence? Because the fact is that you are either climbing or you are sliding. There are no in-betweens, there are no plateaus.

Mark Cuban, the owner of the Dallas Mavericks does many small things for his team that he believes makes a big difference. For example, he provides an excellent team

Never accept the idea that there's a limit to how far you can go.

environment and ensures that his players have a positive experience because he knows that will help them excel as players. So when his team is on the road he makes sure that his players' hotel rooms have oversize beds. This makes them more comfortable, helps them rest better, and improves their attitudes. When they arrive home from away games, he has their cars waiting for them on the airport tarmac, cleaned and polished.

Do Mark Cuban's actions make a difference? Cuban is known as a controversial figure and the media has said a lot of good and bad about him. However, before Cuban bought the Mavericks the public and media considered them the dogs of the NBA, one of the worst teams ever. Now, the Mavericks are one of the best teams in the league. In 2006 they made it to the final game of the NBA championship. Before the 2007 season, Cuban renegotiated the Mavericks's coach Avery Johnson's contract and increased his salary. Johnson had led the team to their best season ever and Cuban knew he needed to reward Johnson's commitment to excellence. Cuban understands that he doesn't have to do these things as an owner, but he believes it is vital to the team's success for him to show his appreciation for their efforts and to build a commitment to excellence in every way. In turn, his team responds with loyalty and high performance. I expect that the Mavericks will be a top-performing, competitive team for many years to come.

YOU GOTTA STRETCH YOURSELF EVERY DAY

Each of us has had times when we've tapped into that something extra, that something that pushed us beyond our limitations. You can tap into this reserve more consistently; you just gotta stretch yourself a little bit every day. That's what Roger Bannister did. He worked to improve his speed every day—sometimes by only milliseconds. But over the years, the constant stretching paid off.

Most of us want to just hop on an elevator, push a button, and quickly arrive at success. Instead, you have to improve one level at a time; you need to construct a stairway to success. As I've said, the most your mind will accept is a small improvement over your last accomplishment. If your best effort produced ten sales in one week, you should set your next goal to eleven sales in a week.

My father taught me a lesson when I was very young that has remained with me throughout my life: "Good, better, best; never let it rest, until your good is better and your better is best." We can't jump directly from "good" to "best." Instead, there are countless steps of "better" and "better still" until we finally reach a world-class performance level. Your best yesterday may not have been good enough, but if you keep trying, stretching, learning, and growing, then your best tomorrow will be better and may bring you the level of success you desire.

Instead, you have to improve one level at a time; you need to construct a stairway to success.

If you're in sales, you can raise the bar by making just one more contact before lunch. On your way home, follow up on a few leads. Each day, call on one client you've lost or haven't sold to in a while. Just say hello and remind them you're still there if they need anything.

Always reach and strive for the next level and never settle for less than your very best. By raising the bar of your personal expectations every day, you will achieve things you never thought possible.

> **Always reach and strive for the next level and never settle for less than your very best.**

YOU GOTTA HAVE DISCIPLINE

Raising the bar takes discipline . . . and lots of it. Even among athletes who have exceptional physical abilities, surprisingly few have the self-discipline required to hone their skills to a razor's edge and become true all-stars. A well-disciplined athlete is one who attends every practice, works to sharpen skills, and is careful about things like diet and sleep habits. As a result, each day he is able to push just a little bit beyond the previous level.

Likewise, a well-disciplined salesperson will make the number of calls required to get the appointments needed, makes every appointment on time, follows up with each prospect, and fulfills the promises made. The disciplined salesperson does these things whether he feels like it or not—even if it's Friday afternoon and he'd rather play golf.

An essential ingredient to success in any area of life is learning discipline. You already have the ability to succeed in any endeavor you choose. The question is, do you have the self-discipline needed to develop that ability to its full potential? By applying the same principles of discipline that all-star athletes use to your unique talents and abilities, your chances of winning will increase significantly.

> **Discipline is the habit of taking consistent action until one can perform with unconscious competence. Discipline weighs ounces, but regret weighs tons.**
>
> **—Jhoon Rhee, world-renowned tenth-degree black belt**

In fact, you have a much better chance of achieving success than an athlete does. Did you know that the odds of a high school football player making it to the NFL are four thousand to one? Or that only 5 to 6 percent of baseball players drafted will ever play in the major leagues?

As a culture, we do not discipline ourselves. The word "discipline" comes with a negative connotation. Some people view discipline as a lack of freedom. I believe discipline equals freedom, because you know that you're in charge. If you tell yourself you'll do something, you do it. You know you will follow through with your commitments.

There is really no such thing as a totally undisciplined person, even though that phrase is often used. You will always be disciplined—you can either choose to discipline yourself or life will do it for you. It is far better to choose the former. The school of hard knocks will leave you battered and bruised, but self-discipline will prepare you to meet challenges head on and give you the power to overcome them.

Evangelist and former pro baseball player Billy Sunday has a speech titled "Payday Someday." Its basic message is that someday you will either receive a great reward or have to pay a great debt. That's the way it works in life, athletics, and business—your efforts will eventually pay off or your lack of effort will eventually cost you dearly.

If you raise the bar, you'll astound yourself at the results. What if you spent just fifteen minutes a day on improving your performance? Where would you be in a year, two years, five years? Consistently raising the bar isn't easy. It will take tremendous courage, dedication, and a lot of hard work. But you can do it. Learn how to push yourself. Then, every day, push yourself just a little further. Every day, expect just a little bit more from yourself. Look for tangible or measurable improvements. Then you'll begin to realize that if you give a little more, you will know how to raise your own bar to new heights. That's what makes it fun!

To win, you gotta raise the bar.

To raise the bar, you gotta

- Go the extra mile
- Stretch yourself every day
- Have discipline

★ CHAPTER 7 ★

YOU GOTTA SELL YOURSELF

WHETHER WE REALIZE IT or not, everyone is selling something. The teacher sells the students on making good grades and getting an education. The preacher sells the congregation on attending church and receiving salvation. Parents sell their children on being good citizens. And kids always sell their parents on something they want. To see this in action, just tell a kid no and watch the sales campaign begin!

> **Everyone lives by selling something.**
>
> **—Robert Louis Stevenson,**
> **Scottish essayist, poet, and**
> **author of fiction and travel books**

If you want to win and achieve your full potential in life, you gotta sell. Your entire life is a continuous process of communicating, persuading, and influencing other people. Tony Jeary is known as the world's utmost authority on speaking and presentations. In his book *Life Is a Series of Presentations*, he convincingly states that the average person makes hundreds of presentations a day. Anytime you communicate with someone—whether it's in business or at home, via email or face-to-face—you're making a presentation. And each of these presentations can have an impact on your life and future. I think anytime you make a presentation, you're trying to sell someone on something, even if it's as simple as selling someone on your idea or opinion.

Even athletes sell. Star athletes sell style, skills, and showmanship. Through their performances, they sell people on the idea that they're the best, and because of this, they create great excitement. Because people recognize them as winners, they want to buy the products they endorse and tickets to watch them play their respective sports. But a star athlete must also continually sell himself to himself to consistently perform at the highest level. If superstar athletes' confidence slips, they lose their edge and their performance suffers.

Selling yourself is a critical factor that determines the level of success you will ultimately achieve and how quickly you will achieve it. You should network, market yourself, and get your name out there. When you promote yourself to others (in an appropriate way), more opportunities will come your way and you'll have better "luck." Of course, it won't be luck at all. Good things will happen to you because people will recognize you and your abilities. When companies downsize, who typically stays? The people who have marketed themselves, their results, and their value to the company. Selling yourself is a universal need.

Good things will happen to you because people will recognize you and your abilities.

Selling yourself involves two steps: First, it means selling others on you and your products or services. But it also means selling you to you. You've got to believe 100 percent in yourself, your abilities, and whatever it is you represent. How can you sell others on you if you're not first sold on yourself? I'm not talking about having a big ego. I'm talking about totally convincing yourself that you are the best person for the job or that the person you're exchanging with is getting a good deal. To sell to others, you gotta be sold on yourself and believe that you have the knowledge, skills, and abilities to achieve success.

YOU GOTTA BELIEVE

Selling in its most basic form is only a transfer of belief. It's sharing what you wholeheartedly believe with others and letting them share in your belief and excitement.

How is it that two people selling the same product, for the same company, in the same territory, working the same hours, can consistently get significantly different results? It's because one person has a strong belief in his abilities and his product, and the other one doesn't.

All superstars believe they're going to be successful. They believe it with their minds and their hearts. When Michael Jordan was in a game, do you think he believed he was going to miss his next shot? How about Tiger Woods: When he's at the tee, does he believe he's going to slice the ball? No way. He has no doubt in his mind he's going to make the perfect shot every single time. Of course, not every shot is "all net" or a hole-in-one, but the person who combines skill with belief usually succeeds.

All superstars believe they're going to be successful.

When top salespeople make a sales call, they never say, "I might sell something today" or "I hope someone buys." Instead, they say, "I know someone is going to buy what I'm selling today. I have a product/opportunity/service I believe in. The prospects have money, and I'm going to trade my belief and enthusiasm for their money."

If you wanted to sell your boss on the idea of giving you a raise, would you know without a shadow of a doubt that you're worth every penny? Or would you feel lucky if you got anything because you don't think you deserve it? If you expect to achieve great things, you gotta believe 100 percent in you!

I'm not a psychologist or a neuroscientist; however, both my research and my personal experiences have shown me that our beliefs about ourselves can actually manifest in physical reality. Your belief dictates your behavior. If you believe you will succeed, you will. If you believe you will fail, then failure is certain. What you believe to be true about yourself is rendered true because of the link between your belief and your actions.

When you have a strong enough belief in yourself, you will release the positive power of belief and transfer that belief to others in a very natural way. As a result, you will dramatically improve your chances of achieving the outcome you desire.

YOU GOTTA RIDE FOR THE BRAND

I strongly believe that anyone who represents a product, service, company, or organization must be loyal to that product, service, company, or organization. Years ago, when cowboys worked on ranches, they called this "riding for the brand." Each ranch had its own brand, such as "Bar 2" or "101." But the brand was more than just a way to mark cattle. It symbolized the ranch and the qualities that ranch represented, and it also symbolized the cowboys as individuals. The cowboys were fiercely loyal and committed to their brand and were willing to stand up for it.

In professional sports, many athletes have sponsors. These are the brands they represent, and the companies expect them to use and demonstrate loyalty to the companies' products and services. If Tiger Woods were a spokesperson for a certain brand of golf balls, he should use their balls exclusively. What would people have thought if Michael Jordan promoted Nike shoes but played in Reeboks? He would have lost credibility with buyers and most likely his endorsement contract with Nike.

Riding for the brand creates credibility, and if you aren't credible, you're going to have a hard time selling yourself—to you or others.

> **Loyalty is something you give regardless of what you get back. In giving loyalty, you're getting more loyalty; and out of loyalty flow other great qualities.**
>
> **—Charlie "Tremendous" Jones, legendary author and speaker**

In sales, riding for the brand goes much deeper than just loyalty to the products or services. You gotta also be loyal to your company, your customers, and yourself. You should never represent or sell anything to anyone unless you truly believe customers will make the best choice by spending their hard-earned money to purchase your product. How can you convince customers they will get the best deal if you haven't spent your own money to buy and use the product? Would you expect to become a top Ford salesperson if you drove a Chevrolet?

Let's pose that question from the buyer's perspective: Would you buy a Ford if you looked over and saw the salesperson's Chevrolet sitting in the parking lot? Probably not.

You'd think, "If this salesperson doesn't think a Ford is good enough to drive, why should I buy one?"

I've never seen anyone make it to the top who wasn't completely loyal to the products, services, organization, idea, philosophy, or cause she represented. Why would you waste your time and energy on something you don't or can't believe in?

If you don't believe in and support the products or company you're involved with, you're a hypocrite, and everyone will know it. You shouldn't ask other people to do something you won't do. You can fake it for a while, but you won't reach your highest potential as long as you're pretending. Riding for the brand is still the only way to gain lasting credibility.

Why would you waste your time and energy on something you don't or can't believe in?

YOU GOTTA CREATE WIN-WIN SITUATIONS

It's easy to be enthusiastic when you represent a product, service, or cause that creates a win-win situation for everyone involved. When a sale is made, the salesperson always gets a win—he makes a commission.

Creating win-win situations is really about giving a little more than you expect to receive.

But to create a win-win, the customer must also win. Customers win when they've acquired a useful or valuable product or service—something that saves them time or money or offers peace of mind and safety. Top producers consistently strive to give each customer a bigger win than the one they receive. In other words, long after they've spent their commission, top producers should ensure that their customers still receive the benefits of the product or service.

Creating win-win situations is really about giving a little more than you expect to receive. In sales, this might mean always making sure that your prices are fair for the products and services you sell or doing your best to ensure that your customers or clients get the best deal possible. This type of effort will benefit you in the long run even if it doesn't benefit you in an immediate way.

Look for the win-win situation in everything you do. Then work to make it happen. It's not hard to get excited about representing something if you know the other party always wins because of your efforts.

YOU GOTTA LOVE WHAT YOU DO

When I made the decision to stick it out in sales, financial reasons were not the determining factors. I made my decision through careful evaluation of what I liked—and didn't like—about this kind of work. I found that sales is the best profession for me because there are more things about it that I like than dislike. I love the fact that I have the opportunity to meet so many different people. I also love that I can set my own hours, determine my income, and have unlimited potential to advance. To me, sales means freedom!

> **Selling is essentially a transference of feelings.**
>
> **—Zig Ziglar, author and motivational speaker**

To achieve the highest level of success and perform at your peak ability, you gotta love what you do. Otherwise, you will become easily sidetracked. You won't stick with it through the inevitable tough times, and you won't consistently take the actions necessary to succeed.

If you don't love what you do, you have two choices: You can either change what you do, or you can change what you love. Oftentimes, you'll be better off figuring out what you love about what you do than changing careers. Why? Because no matter what you do, you'll always be able to find something you don't like about it. But that doesn't necessarily mean that it's not the right career for you.

I once read a story about Benjamin Franklin. It said that Franklin made decisions by taking a piece of paper and writing all the reasons to do something on one side and all the reasons not to do it on the other. Then he would evaluate both sides and make his decision based on the results.

I challenge you to do the same. Take a sheet of paper and draw a line down the middle. On one side, write everything you love about your career. Then, on the other side, write everything you don't like. Now, evaluate both sides. Most of the time, you will find more things that you like than dislike. But you can't just look at the number of reasons on each side—you also have to evaluate the relative meaning and impact of each reason. For example, you might have three positives and five negatives. But the three positives may be huge, quality-of-life issues, whereas the five negatives are minor administrative headaches you could learn to live with.

This exercise will help you discover what motivates and excites you. When you focus on the positives, the negatives will become insignificant. And as you focus on your likes, you will love what you do even more. The more you love what you do, the more you win.

If you come to the realization that you truly don't like what you do or that you can't live with the negatives, you need to start looking for an exit strategy. Find something you do love, and I'd be willing to bet you'll be successful at it.

Remember, the most important sale you'll ever make is to sell yourself on who you are and what you do. The toughest prospect you'll ever have is you. If you can sell you, you've got it made.

To win, you gotta sell yourself.

To sell yourself, you gotta

- Believe
- Ride for the brand
- Create win-win situations
- Love what you do

★ CHAPTER 8 ★

YOU GOTTA BE A
STRAIGHT SHOOTER

IF YOU WANT TO WIN long-term, you gotta be a straight shooter. You gotta have character and integrity; you gotta be honest, forthright, ethical, and trustworthy.

> **If you believe in unlimited quality and act in all your business dealings with total integrity, the rest will take care of itself.**
>
> **—Frank Perdue, pioneer in the poultry business**

While a quality like honesty is fairly straightforward—either you lie, steal, or cheat, or you don't—the concept of integrity is not so cut and dried. As with the concept of success, integrity means different things to different people because it is linked to personal values. As a result, people judge others' integrity based on their own value system.

However, I think there is a certain level of integrity we can all agree on. Integrity is about living up to the standards of your profession, calling, or position. It means being trustworthy, even when no one will ever find out what you've done. It's easy to have integrity when someone is watching. The true test is what you do when no one is around.

Character, on the other hand, goes deeper. Character is about who you are as a person. Character is the ability to follow through with a commitment, goal, or dream long after the excitement of the moment is gone. Integrity influences your behavior, while character is about who you are and where you're going. Being a straight shooter means putting your character into action and living a life of integrity.

YOU GOTTA MAINTAIN YOUR INTEGRITY

Maintaining your integrity often becomes a critical issue when you succeed because it is then that you may be called upon to compromise your principles. In order to truly win, you gotta keep your integrity despite your success.

> **Integrity is not a 90 percent thing, not a 95 percent thing; either you have it or you don't.**
>
> **—Peter Scotese, industrialist**

Developing a reputation for honesty and integrity is something you should strive for simply because it's the right thing to do, but it's also a smart business and sales strategy. People do business with people they like and trust. When you have integrity, your prospects, customers, peers, and coworkers will trust you. And the more people trust you, the less risk they feel in working with you and in buying from you.

The truly outstanding salesperson is the one who doesn't misrepresent what the product or service can do. The salesperson with integrity tells prospects when a product or service isn't right for them. Even if a prospect doesn't buy, he or she will always remember the salesperson's integrity. According to Zig Ziglar, "The most important persuasion tool you have in your entire arsenal is integrity."

Don't get me wrong—I've made some mistakes I'm not proud of. What I can tell you is that the agony, dissatisfaction, and other negative consequences the low road brought were never worth it. I learned that lesson the hard way. Now I do my best to avoid the low road no matter what instant satisfaction or temporary rewards it may seem to offer. Taking the high road is often not easy or popular, but if you compromise your principles and integrity, it will always end up costing you in the long run.

YOU GOTTA PLAY BY THE RULES

Sometimes in the game of life, people become frustrated because they're not achieving their goals fast enough. The success they desire seems so far away. Instead of working harder, they give in to the temptation to cut corners and bend—or even break—the rules. Their desire for success overrides their sense of right and wrong, and they mistakenly think success is worth more than their integrity.

Then there are people who have achieved a certain level of success and think they are above the rules. Many of these individuals followed the rules to get to the top; but once they got there, they felt the rules didn't apply to them anymore. They believe they can continue to ignore the rules and they won't experience any consequences, but it's only a matter of time before they get caught.

People who break the rules either to achieve success or because they have achieved a certain level of success have walked away from integrity. They stop relying on their moral compasses to keep them on track. I'm always amazed at all-stars who sabotage themselves. Success throws them out of their comfort zones, and they start making bad decisions. In the 1988 Olympics, Canadian sprinter Ben Johnson roared past the competition, broke the world record in the 100 meters, and won the gold medal. But when he tested positive for steroids, he was forced to forfeit his medal and his record was erased. His gold was given to the silver medalist, American Carl Lewis.

People who break the rules either to achieve success or because they have achieved a certain level of success have walked away from integrity.

Investigators later discovered that Johnson had used steroids for several years to improve his performance. He had succumbed to the promise of fame and success that comes with being a world champion. And because he had gotten away with it, he continued to break the rules. The saddest part of the story is that Johnson was eventually banned from the sport. Imagine how different his life could have been if only he had played by the rules.

Just as there are no shortcuts to success in sports, there are no shortcuts to success in life, business, or sales. If you're frustrated because you're not achieving your goals fast enough, don't give in to the temptation to break the rules. That's not the answer. You may achieve some short-term success, but your lapse of integrity will come back to haunt you. Instead, go to your coach for advice, change your strategy if necessary, and then work harder.

YOU GOTTA FOLLOW THROUGH

To be a straight shooter, you have to do what you say you're going to do. You can't say one thing and then do another. There's a big difference between people who are interested and those who are committed. People who are committed will do whatever it takes to follow through.

It's been said that you are only as good as your word. Actually, I think this is only half right. I think it should be, "You are only as good as your word—if you do what you say you will do." Your word must be your bond. If you commit to something, follow through. A person who keeps his or her word every time will gain respect from others. But a person who doesn't keep his or her word, even in little things, will earn a negative reputation.

There's a big difference between people who are interested and those who are committed.

People often think that if they have good intentions they are straight shooters. That's simply not true. You can have all the good intentions in the world, but if you don't act in a way that's consistent with those intentions, your goodwill is meaningless. The following quote from the book *Walk the Talk* illustrates how our actions are more meaningful than our intentions: "We judge ourselves mostly by our intentions, but others judge us mostly by our actions. People hear what we say, but they see what we do. And seeing is believing."

You keep customers by delivering on your promises, fulfilling your commitments, and continually investing in the quality of your relationships.

—Cavett Robert, founder of the National Speakers Association

To stay in the game, you gotta deliver what you promise. And walking the talk is absolutely critical in sales. I've seen a lot of companies with good products that are no longer in business because they didn't follow through on their commitments. In sports, if you don't deliver, you'll get cut from the team. In business, you must absolutely deliver on the commitments and obligations you make to customers, even if it means working overtime or losing money. Your ability and willingness to follow through and walk your talk are key indicators of your success.

Some people have a hard time honoring their commitments simply because they haven't learned when and how to say no. They make too many promises without thinking about how they're going to fulfill those commitments. This is the type of short-term thinking that gets people in trouble. It is far better to make fewer commitments and keep the ones you do make than to agree to everything and only partially deliver on the promise.

Following through is simply the right thing to do, but it also has an unexpected benefit. When you follow through on your commitments (including the commitments you make to yourself), you gain confidence, belief, and momentum.

YOU GOTTA BE HONEST WITH YOURSELF

Being a straight shooter and following through goes much further than being honest with others. To be a straight shooter you must be completely honest with yourself. You are the most important person to be honest with because self-awareness is the key to improving any area of your life or business.

You are also the toughest person to be honest with. Why? Because it's difficult to admit that there are areas of our lives where we're falling short and not living up to the standards we've set for ourselves. To admit there's a problem implies that we should do something about it and that throws us out of our comfort zones. So, we take the path of least resistance and either ignore our problems or rationalize them away. But the rationalizations you give yourself are exactly what keep you from becoming the person you were destined to be. When you rationalize, you try to justify to yourself and others that there are good, valid reasons why you act or behave the way you do.

If you're going to win, you gotta be honest with yourself and admit there are some things that must change. You gotta stop rationalizing and get a crystal clear understanding of where you truly stand in all areas of your life and business. Self-honesty is the cure for rationalizations. In short, you gotta stop sugarcoating your lack of achievement and your problems and face them head on!

When you settle for less than who you could be, you settle for a life of mediocrity . . . and winners aren't mediocre.

> **Most people never run far enough on their first wind to find out they've got a second.**
>
> **—William James, philosopher, author, and lecturer**

So stop right now and do a gut check. Get rid of the sugarcoating and rationalizations and face the hard truth about your hang-ups. See things as they really are. If you're like me, thinking about these things probably makes you uncomfortable . . .

that's the whole idea. The purpose of this process is to show you the truth, help you break these destructive patterns, and give you the power and the inspiration to change.

On a piece of paper, write down the answers to the following questions.

1. **What issues keep you from being all that you know deep inside you can be?** Consider characteristics, traits, negative habits, poor business practices. What actions or behaviors are inconsistent with the standards and values you've set for yourself personally and professionally? In which areas are you not working hard enough or not committed enough? Which aspects of your life are just not good enough anymore?

2. **What rationalizations and reasons do you give yourself for staying in the middle of your mess?** How do you sugarcoat your problems and hang-ups?

3. **What are the reasons why you must stop these rationalizations and break the negative patterns that are holding you back?** Because you know you can do or be so much more? To take your company or team to the next level? Because your family deserves it? Knowing why you must do something gives you the power and commitment to follow through and make the change.

4. **What kind of person do you have to become to move past these issues and achieve the life that most people only dream about?** What characteristics, qualities, and beliefs must you develop? What actions must you take on a consistent basis? How must you think, talk, act, believe, and behave? How must you treat the people in your life? How confident must you be?

Now, become that person! Go out and act as if you are this new you. Decide right now to be that person—a person who can do what it takes to win.

Your biggest opponent is yourself and your rationalizations. If you continue to face the truth every day, if you demand more of yourself than other people expect, if you keep your integrity and play by the rules, and if you follow through on your commitments, life will reward you accordingly. Not only will you usually win, but you will do so with a clean conscience. You will have earned self-respect and the respect of others, and you'll feel good about the success you have achieved.

To win, you gotta be a straight shooter.

To be a straight shooter, you gotta

- Maintain your integrity
- Play by the rules
- Follow through
- Be honest with yourself

★ CHAPTER 9 ★

YOU GOTTA BE COACHABLE

WHILE YOUR SKILLS and your willingness to work hard are important, you will succeed much faster if you are coachable. Being coachable means you are willing to listen to, take advice from, and learn from those who have more experience than you do. If you are coachable, you can learn virtually all of the skills you need to win the game.

> In order to excel, you must be . . . prepared to work hard and be willing to accept constructive criticism.
>
> —Willie Mays, professional baseball hall of famer

One of the greatest things a coach can say about a player is that he or she is coachable. Teachers love to find students who are eager to learn. Sales managers get excited when they find trainees who are eager to grow in the organization. Unfortunately, too many people consider themselves hotshots—they feel invincible and think they already know all the strategies for success. As a result, they won't listen to people who have more experience and wisdom than they do. There is an old adage that says, "Learn from the mistakes of others, because life isn't long enough to make them all yourself."

YOU GOTTA LISTEN SO YOU CAN LEARN

Listening is a critical part of your long-term success. If you don't listen, you can't learn. And if you want to earn more, you gotta learn more. I've always heard, "If you keep doing what you've always done, you'll keep getting what you've always gotten."

Continuous learning is the key to superstardom. The highest-paid professionals in any field spend more money improving themselves than the average individuals who just get by. This means they constantly listen to self-improvement audio programs, to top performers at seminars, and to the wisdom found in books.

It marks a big step in your development when you come to realize that other people can help you do a better job than you could do alone.

—Andrew Carnegie, industrialist and entrepreneur

If you are willing to listen, you will learn what works and, just as importantly, what doesn't work. Take advantage of the wisdom of your managers, leaders, and mentors—it will help you avoid costly mistakes and unnecessary setbacks.

I see many top salespeople join a sales force and start out with a bang. The ideas and techniques they use work well, and they achieve some initial success. Then, somewhere along the way, they start to think success is easy. They stop listening, and they find ways to cut corners. Many of them don't even realize they've changed, but the shortcuts eventually catch up with them and they fall into a slump. This is the time when they must refocus, get back to the basics, quit taking shortcuts, and start listening to their coaches.

There are many ideas and techniques you may want to try throughout your career that have already been tried, tested, and shown to fail. Your coach can guide you safely past these landmines, but you gotta listen. If you don't, you could do great damage to yourself and possibly to others by spending too much time, energy, and effort in areas that will lead to certain failure. I learned that lesson the hard way.

One of my biggest challenges in sales management occurred shortly after I was promoted to sales director. I was doing incredibly well. We had just achieved the status of number one sales team in the world, and I had promoted five of our top salespeople to open their own offices. I couldn't have been doing better . . . or so I thought!

While attending my first directors' meeting, I discovered that I was being undermined by one of the top producers I had promoted. He was going behind my back telling others in the company that he was the reason for my team's success and that without him our team wouldn't survive. I had a choice to make: I could try to solve this problem on my own, or I could listen to the advice and wisdom of the other directors. I chose to listen and learn.

At that meeting, I received a lot of good advice and some constructive criticism. The other directors let me know I actually had quite a few problems in my organization and that I had many challenges ahead of me. They also told me it probably wasn't the smartest move to have promoted my top five salespeople all in the same year. I learned that I needed to stay in closer contact with the people in my organization and to keep my ear to the ground. Because my peers were kind enough to share personal experiences about how they overcame similar challenges—and because I was willing to listen and learn—I went home with some different strategies and a new plan to take our organization to the next level.

That year I worked harder and smarter than ever before. I invested more time, effort, and energy in the individuals in our organization. I let the team know I was coachable, and they knew without a doubt that I was in the game. Because of my actions, I earned their support. That year we were able to once again become number one, and we broke three long-standing production records—all without the salespeople I had promoted the year before.

The moral of the story is this: I went to that first directors' meeting feeling a little invincible. I was a twenty-two-year-old rookie making incredible money and living life to its fullest. Because I was on top, I could have easily let my ego get in the way and not listened to the older, more experienced directors. Instead, I did listen and I gained invaluable experience.

I think I also earned the respect of my colleagues, not only as someone who would listen, but also as someone who would take action based on the advice given to him. In short, I proved I was coachable.

The failures I've experienced in my career have taught me that each level of success requires more commitment and a greater willingness to listen and learn. There is no such thing as "arriving" or "making it." Many people have a good year, and suddenly you can't tell them anything. I'm always disappointed to see that happen, because it's a condition that will eventually send them back to the starting gates.

There is no such thing as "arriving" or "making it."

YOU GOTTA HAVE THE RIGHT COACH

Any superstar athlete will tell you that you gotta find the right coach. Studies have shown that having the right coach or mentor can make all the difference in your performance. If I worked in the computer industry, I would want Bill Gates or Michael Dell as my mentor and coach. I would want to tap into the knowledge and wisdom that got them to the top of their game.

You can, and should, take the same approach. Every avenue of life has its superstars. Seek them out. Spend time with them and ask them questions. Find out how they became so successful. Pick their brains and learn their pattern or model for success. Get to know how they think and what makes them tick. The reality is this: if you ask the right people the right questions, you will get the right answers. These relationships can offer you a wealth of knowledge and the opportunity to improve yourself by implementing the same strategies that have made others so successful.

> **Learn from the legends, watch the top players, and apply tactics that work for them to your own game.**
>
> **—Brad Gilbert, coach to top tennis professionals**

You may wonder how to find the right coach. You need to realize that you have people in your life right now who can mentor you. They will have unique talents and skills that you will want to emulate. Find those individuals who are the highest performers in your area of interest. You don't want counsel from someone who's only been involved in that endeavor for a year or two. Seek out individuals whom you admire and respect and can relate to. When considering whether someone is the right coach for you, ask yourself the following questions:

- Is this someone I am willing to tell my commitments to?
- Is this someone I would share my failures and successes with?
- Is this someone who will lead me by example and someone I will follow?
- Will this person hold me to a higher standard and not let me off the hook?
- Will I follow through with this person even if it is uncomfortable or difficult?

Take time now to write down the names of three to five individuals you know (or would like to know) who possess the characteristics you want in a coach. Even if you don't know them, write them down for two reasons. First, if you're willing to work hard enough, you can meet anyone on the planet you want to meet. You may have heard of the theory of six degrees of separation. The concept—which has been tested and proven—is that anyone on Earth can connect to any other person through a chain of acquaintances that has no more than six links. But even if you don't have the time to go through the effort of meeting the people on your list, there are likely numerous sources of information (articles, books, audio programs, seminars, websites) by or about them that you can access. Use these sources to study their attitudes, work habits, and belief systems, and then duplicate them.

Many people have asked me how they should ask someone to become their mentor. My answer is that you shouldn't.

First and foremost, having a mentor is an internal decision on your part. It's about observing and learning from others. The external part of coaching involves seeking out individuals you want to emulate and then gradually establishing a relationship with them. Don't go up to someone you barely know and ask them to become your mentor and spend a lot of time helping you. Instead, over a period of time, ask them questions about themselves and how they became successful. This will help you develop some rapport. Eventually you will feel the time is right to ask them if they will share some of their strategies for success with you.

> **We could all use a little coaching. When you're playing the game, it's hard to think of everything.**
>
> **—Jim Rohn, author and legendary motivational speaker**

I do have one warning for you when it comes to finding the right coach: Be careful whom you associate with and listen to. Find successful mentors you can look up to who will guide you. Now you might think that's obvious, but it would surprise you to know how many people take advice from mediocre performers or from family and friends who don't have "the fruit on the tree." Every time I attend a meeting or seminar I see the same thing: A top salesperson is on stage giving advice about how he or she achieved success. I walk out into the hall and see a group of people in the corner, and the person who has sold the least is giving everyone else advice on how to sell! This is the same person who has bill collectors calling, has four bald tires on his car, and is selling less today than he was five years ago. It always amazes me that there are people willing to listen to him.

If you were to ask me what I believe is the single most important success principle that has helped me throughout my career, my answer would be simply, "I am coachable." Almost everything I know about sales and life in general I have learned from mentors and coaches, whether I got it from spending time with the person or indirectly from books or audio programs. I understand there are people who know a lot more than I do, and I'm always anxious to discover what it is.

> **If you were to ask me what I believe is the single most important success principle that has helped me throughout my career, my answer would be simply, "I am coachable."**

Even if you're successful and winning the game, you still need to be coachable and listen to and learn from people with a proven track record. In Michael Jordan's book *For the Love of the Game*, he makes a comment regarding the idea that he was the greatest basketball player of all time: "I built my talents on the shoulders of someone else's talents . . . I have used all the great players who came before me to improve my skills . . . I listened, I was aware of my success, but I never stopped trying to get better." He was able to achieve truly unprecedented success by learning from those who had achieved success before him. If it worked for Michael Jordan, it can work for you.

To win, you gotta be coachable.

To be coachable, you gotta

- Listen so you can learn
- Have the right coach

★ CHAPTER 10 ★

YOU GOTTA HAVE A TEAM

TO WIN IN ANY GAME takes teamwork. Even athletes in individual sports are part of a team. Every successful boxer has a trainer, a manager, a sponsor, and a gym. A victorious racecar driver needs a pit crew, a sponsor, and a car owner. World-class gymnasts have trainers.

> **Coming together is a beginning; keeping together is progress; working together is success.**
>
> **—Henry Ford, inventor and automobile pioneer**

No matter what you want to accomplish, it will be virtually impossible to achieve all-star status unless you work with a team. You don't win championships by yourself. You will need the help and support of others to reach your goals. And to win in sales, you need a good company behind you, a dedicated service department, and an effective leader.

Chances are, Michael Jordan would not have achieved such long-term, spectacular fame without a team of winners around him. His team made him better, and in turn, he made them better. He passed off many game-winning shots to his teammates; but because his team won, he won. A great player needs a great team just as much as a great team needs great players.

YOU GOTTA BE A TEAM PLAYER

To win consistently, you gotta be a team player. What does it mean to be a team player? It means communicating and cooperating with others. It's about being patient and being open to the ideas of other people, even people who may be very different from you. Team players are solution oriented—they help create win-win situations for everybody involved. And team players share leadership responsibilities and accountabilities.

> **One person seeking glory doesn't accomplish much. Success is a result of people pulling together to meet common goals.**
>
> **—John Maxwell, author and leadership expert**

When I am on a team, I have to learn how to blend in and work with others. I cannot be self-centered or interested only in results that meet my personal objectives. In some ways, I must lose my "self" and my selfishness as I come together with others to achieve something I could not achieve on my own. With a team around me, I can win!

When you're part of a team, your individual goals become subservient to the team's objectives. We see this mentality throughout successful businesses and sports teams. Team players know that being on a team is a two-way street. You see, a team will only be successful if every team member is willing to give and take. If you want to receive support from others, you have to give support. If people are there just to get, it never works. Always keep in mind Zig Ziglar's famous saying from his book *See You at the Top*: "You can have everything in life you want if you will just help enough other people get what they want."

I believe that to totally fulfill ourselves in our professional and personal lives we must connect with others and contribute to their success and well-being. I've always heard that if you get to the top of Success Mountain by yourself, you'll probably end up jumping off.

YOU GOTTA KNOW YOUR ROLE

An essential part of being a team player and helping your team win is knowing what role or position you're expected to play. As you learn to adapt to each role and become successful at it, your role on the team will change. As time goes by, the role you play will become bigger and more important.

> **None of us is more important than the rest of us.**
>
> —Ray Kroc, philanthropist and founder of McDonald's Corporation

When I started in sales, I knew nothing about the industry, so it would have been silly for me to try to create my own team. Fortunately, I was able to join a winning team and contribute to its success. As my skills and confidence increased, so did my role, and I became a bigger part of the team. Over the years, as I gained valuable experience and knowledge, I began to assume various leadership duties. Eventually, I became president and chief operating officer of the company. Obviously, there was no way I could have started out at this level. I had to start with small roles and work my way up to larger ones. At each point along the way, I knew I had a certain position to play to ensure the team's success. I took each role seriously, had pride in my position, and worked hard.

Just as in sports, there aren't always enough positions to fill for everyone on the team. Some people aren't willing to accept the role the coach wants them to play. They don't realize the coach understands the bigger, long-term picture and has the best interests of the team in mind. As a result, their negativity creates disharmony on the team. People who aren't willing to play the position the team needs them to play will eventually be replaced.

Sometimes you're better off playing a role that's different from the one you want. You may be asked to play a role you don't even feel you're good at, but you have to realize you've been given this role for a reason. Frequently, taking on a different position or project can be a tremendous boost to your career.

No matter what position your team asks you to play, give it your all. Know that you're contributing in a very important way to the overall success of the team. Remember: When the team wins, you win.

YOU GOTTA BE A LITTLE "POLITICAL"

Let's face it—if you're involved in any group or team, you're going to have to deal with some amount of politics. That's just the way it is. But if you're aware of the political elements in any given situation, your success will bloom at a faster rate.

I know a lot of people who never seem to achieve success. They often talk negatively about their company or their teammates, and they don't buy into their company's philosophy, vision, or leadership. This is their downfall because their leader and company can never rely on them. They don't realize they are their own worst enemy.

To be successful, you gotta publicly support your team's mission and stand behind your leader and teammates. Do you support your teammates? Do you cheer them on and celebrate their successes and accomplishments? Or do you tend to spread unfortunate news and pass along the latest gossip? If you have hurt someone through your gossip, be a big enough person to apologize. Then guard against making the same mistake in the future by getting your gossiping under control.

In your dealings with others, remember to praise in public, but criticize only in private. You should discuss any

To be successful, you gotta publicly support your team's mission and stand behind your leader and teammates.

problems behind closed doors and keep this information among the people you trust most. Leaks of sensitive information can be extremely destructive. Loose lips do sink ships. Never forget that you and your teammates are all in the same boat.

YOU GOTTA BUILD UP THE TEAM

Building up your teammates through your words and actions is a key principle for winning. It creates a protective shield or barrier around the team and the organization. When people build up each other, help each other find success, they create an unbreakable bond, a bond they will need to make it through tough times.

Having supportive team members is a key reason why some teams and organizations flourish and thrive while others don't. Teams are built or destroyed by words and actions. If you pay close attention, you'll notice that members of championship teams always support each other. Team members constantly give credit to other players, the coaches, owners, and sponsors.

The opposite is also true: When people speak poorly of their teammates or the organization, the team breaks down.

We see it all too often in sports—a player says something negative about another player or the coach to the media. That usually prompts the "attacked" person to fire back with something negative, and a downward spiral begins.

Teams are built or destroyed by words and actions.

We all have the power to choose each and every day whether we will build others up or tear them down; whether we will gossip, gripe, and complain, or work to build a strong and powerful team. It takes careful thought and planning to support and build your team and teammates. It takes very little time to destroy. If more people focused on helping others find success, we would have a lot more successful people in the world, and it would be a better place to live.

Building up others doesn't mean saying things you don't believe are true or agreeing with everything someone says or does. It's about finding the good qualities that exist in others and then focusing on and talking about those positive points. No one is perfect and everyone makes mistakes. Praise and recognize others for the good they do and tolerate the characteristics that make each of us less than perfect.

Praise and recognize others for the good they do and tolerate the characteristics that make each of us less than perfect.

Unfortunately, looking for the positives doesn't come naturally for most of us. We've become conditioned to look for the negative in every situation. But with some practice, we can all become experts in supporting our team. Here are five steps to help you focus on building up others:

1. **Encourage** Everyone loves to be encouraged. Make a conscious effort to be more positive towards others—lift them up, help them feel more confident and secure, and let them know how important they are to you.

2. **Educate** If you want people to grow and become better at what they do, consistently give them positive, constructive feedback and provide them with the best tools available to help them win.

3. **Celebrate** Find ways to recognize achievements with meaningful awards and ceremonies. Create an atmosphere where people want to become successful. This is fun for everyone and is a great way to build unity and motivate the team.

4. **Console** Be alert to the problems and needs that surround you. Care about people. Be willing to listen to their problems, hurts and pains, and then build them back up.

5. **Communicate** Effective communication is the key to the first four steps. Remember: it's not what you say that matters; it's how your people receive the message. If the person you're trying to communicate with doesn't hear the message you intended to give, you haven't communicated effectively.

If you want to reach the highest level of success, you gotta learn to tap into the amazing power of supporting your teammates. It is the oil that keeps a successful team running smoothly. It creates positive, excited, belief-oriented teams. Learn to give it and receive it well. You will quickly discover that when you build others up, they will begin to build you up in return. Do it now, and you will see the benefits in the months and years to come.

YOU GOTTA CREATE TEAM SYNERGY

There is amazing power in teams. It's that mysterious, almost magical quality called synergy. As it relates to teams, synergy means the interaction of two or more people so that their combined output is greater than the sum of their individual

Teamwork creates synergy, and synergy creates excitement and magnification.

efforts and talents. In other words, with synergy 1 + 1 + 1 + 1 equals a lot more than 4! The magic comes in the "+" sign that joins people together and encourages us to achieve more than we could on our own. Teamwork creates synergy, and synergy creates excitement and magnification.

Pretend for a moment that you're at the biggest championship game of the year. Your team is at home and winning. As the clock ticks down to the final seconds, thousands of screaming, cheering, excited fans are going nuts. Every part of your body is vibrating, and your endorphins are flowing.

Now imagine the same game, at the same moment, but this time there are only four other fans in the entire stadium. When your team wins, how would the experience feel? You may say, "It's great—I'd have the best seats in the house." But the truth is, if there are only five people yelling "Yeah!" it's not quite the same.

Think about it: How does any event feel when you experience it on your own? I can guarantee it's not nearly as much fun as experiencing it with other people. When you experience success as a team, your team members' excitement adds to your excitement. You could never experience that same level of excitement alone. That's the power of synergy.

Team synergy comes from the capacity to work with and share with others at a deep level on a continuous basis.

Teamwork in business is about sharing—sharing work, ideas, opinions, knowledge, thoughts, and feelings. By definition, team membership means sharing yourself with others and being willing to receive from others. Team synergy comes from the capacity to work with and share with others at a deep level on a continuous basis. Some of these relationships will help you grow like you've never grown before. Some will be difficult and make you look at your skills and talents from a new perspective. Some will give you a tremendous sense of contribution. And some will expand your capacity to achieve excellence at a level you never could have accomplished alone.

There is a connection that happens between people when they share. That connection creates the energy that produces results greater than the sum of the individual efforts. When you share as a team, you magnify all that is good. When there is synergy, there is expansion and magnification.

You will never experience success at the same level of intensity and joy as you will when you achieve victory as a member of a team.

To win, you gotta have a team.

To have a team, you gotta

- Be a team player
- Know your role
- Be a little political
- Build up the team
- Create team synergy

★ CHAPTER 11 ★

YOU GOTTA OVERCOME ADVERSITY

I'VE ALWAYS HEARD that when life knocks you down you need to land on your back, because if you can look up, you can get up. The defining difference between average performers and all-stars is that when all-stars get knocked down, they get back up. They refuse to stay down for long. Although bruised and sometimes wounded, they pick themselves up and start over again.

I almost left this chapter out of the book, but I spend a lot of time traveling around the country and speaking to different audiences and they are overwhelmingly appreciative that I discuss the subject of adversity with them. I believe that I get this response because of the truth in a saying I once heard: You are either in an adversity, just getting over an adversity, or about to be in an adversity. Frankly, everybody experiences adversity from time to time. I don't care how good you are, bad things sometimes happen to good people.

> **Adversity causes some men to break, others to break records.**
>
> **—William Arthur Ward, author, educator, and motivational speaker**

The world is full of people who claim they could have made it to the big leagues if only they had gotten a lucky break or if only they hadn't received some kind of injury. They could have made it to the top if only the boss wasn't such a jerk, if only they'd had a chance for a better education, if only their family was more supportive. You can "if only" your life away, or you can decide that you want to live above your circumstances. You can decide that your past will not determine your future.

YOU GOTTA KNOW THERE WILL BE BIG CHALLENGES

No one wins every game. Every player has slumps and losing streaks. There is not an athlete on the playing field who hasn't overcome problems, injuries, and personal trials. Most of us don't realize that most successful people faced challenges and setbacks on their way to success. Every salesperson has bad days, bad weeks, and even bad months. Every business has unprofitable quarters. A surprising number of millionaires have been bankrupt at least once in their lives.

We are all going to have times in our lives when we are faced with adversity Some of the problems will be small, and we can deal with them immediately. Others will be much bigger—they have the potential to knock us out of the game and send us to the sidelines. The only difference between temporary setbacks and long-term ones is the amount of downtime you decide to give yourself.

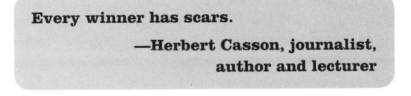

Every winner has scars.

**—Herbert Casson, journalist,
author and lecturer**

I have experienced much adversity in my journey toward success, and I have shared a few of these with you. But none of them can compare to what happened in the year 2000—the sudden death of my young daughter. It was a life-changing event I never could have expected or prepared for; I was very devastated.

Just two weeks prior to her death, I was offered the position of president of my company. Even though my team was doing well, the company as a whole was facing some challenges. Sales were down for the fifth year in a row and down 50 percent from their all-time highs. The company decided it was time for a change, and I was flattered when offered the opportunity to lead the company to better days.

After my daughter's death, I realized I had two choices: I could pick myself up, face my new life, and go on; or I could bail out of the president's job and retreat back to what was safe and comfortable. No one would have blamed me if I'd quit; most people wouldn't even know because my company hadn't announced the new position.

But I chose to pick myself up and go on. I knew I had to find a purpose where there seemed to be none. I had to find out what was really important to me and to my family and use it as my motivation. I became more determined than I had ever been in my entire life. I had one mission, and that was for my family, me, and my company to make it through this tremendously challenging time.

Since then, many people have asked me exactly what I did to overcome such profound adversity. The truth is, I faced the challenges the same way I had confronted so many other obstacles in my life, using the concepts I've outlined in this chapter.

YOU GOTTA LEARN FROM YOUR CHALLENGES

In every challenge, there is a lesson. There is always something you can learn and some way you can become better because of the adversity you face. I've learned that you don't always get a second chance, so you had better make the most of each day and take advantage of every opportunity.

The next time you face a challenge, be it large or small, take a moment to really consider what opportunity lies within the challenge. Ask yourself, "What is good about this challenge?" You may say, "There is nothing good about it at all." So, ask yourself, "What could be good about it?" Even if you can't find anything positive, ask yourself, "What can I learn from this?" You can learn important lessons from every adversity.

In every challenge, there is a lesson.

In sales, if you experience a series of rejections from customers, ask yourself if there are some common elements in all of the situations that might help explain why you aren't closing the deals. Are there some areas you can improve to achieve better results? It's that kind of thought process and analysis that is required if you want to learn from your challenges.

It's important to remember that you have resources available to help you learn from your challenges. Remember, you gotta have a coach and you gotta have a team. Your coach and teammates are great resources for helping you analyze the challenges you're facing. Take your challenges to them and ask their opinions. They probably have some insights you never would have considered on your own.

YOU GOTTA PICK YOURSELF UP

While you can't always control what happens to you, you can control your response. It's not what happens to you in life, it's how you act or react that makes the difference.

When things go wrong or circumstances are beyond your control, don't waste valuable time blaming others for what happened. Shift your attention from what is wrong to what the situation means to your future. Take a step back and realize that tomorrow is another day. Every down is followed by an up. Harness the power of words, thoughts, and actions to make your optimism and faith in the future more real than your difficulties in the present.

> **It is not what happens to you, but how you handle what happens to you that makes the difference.**
>
> **—Zig Ziglar, author and motivational speaker**

I've found that there are ten steps to moving beyond your challenges in the present and turning them into opportunities for a better future:

- Make decisions;
- Set goals;
- Take the first step and then follow up with baby steps every day;
- Raise the bar and raise your standards;
- Work on your attitude every day;
- Rely on your coach and team members;
- Focus on what is right in your life and career and not what is wrong;
- Replace negative thoughts with positive ones;
- Will yourself to stay in the game;

- And, most importantly, pray daily—continually ask God for wisdom and strength.

When you experience adversity (and at some point, everyone will experience adversity), you gotta step back and take time to heal. It's okay to have some downtime, but don't let yourself get in a rut or slump. Be sure to set a date to get back in the game. You must pick yourself up, face your fears head on, examine your priorities, set new objectives and goals, get refocused, and maybe even mend some fences. These simple steps will help you become productive again and get your momentum back.

During the down times, it's crucial that you read inspirational books about overcomers, people who have achieved great things in spite of great challenges and adversities. Listen to motivational audio programs and seek counsel from your coach or mentor.

Sound familiar? I know that the concepts I'm sharing with you in this book work. I know it because I've applied them during the good times of my life and achieved tremendous results. But I also know you can apply them in your worst times, and they will make you stronger and see you through to a new season. As you conquer each challenging day, you will see daylight again. Eventually you will emerge a stronger, more powerful, and more successful person. Remember: the quality of your life is determined by the actions you take.

YOU GOTTA MAKE A COMEBACK

No matter how bad the pain is, if you're willing to make an effort—and at times it may require a fierce effort—you can come back bigger, better, and stronger. Lance Armstrong overcame incredible odds to become a seven-time Tour de France (the most prestigious race in cycling) champion.

Depending on how you choose to react to adversity, it can make you stronger and better, and you can make a comeback.

In 1996, although he had never won the Tour de France, Lance Armstrong was the number one ranked cyclist in the world. But in October of that year, Lance discovered he had advanced testicular cancer that had spread to his lungs and brain. Chances for his recovery were less than 50 percent. He endured two surgeries, including brain surgery, and chemotherapy. Although he was weak, Lance started to think about racing again only five months after his diagnosis. Unfortunately, to add insult to injury, his sponsor had dropped him.

But Lance didn't let that stop him. He decided to make a comeback. In 1998, he declared victory over cancer and returned to racing. The road back was long and hard, with many challenges and discouragements. But just one year later, in 1999, Lance won the Tour de France. Amazingly, he is now the only person in history to have won the race seven years in a row. What a comeback!

The question is, if Lance Armstrong had never experienced the adversity of cancer, would he have become the greatest cyclist in history? In his book *Every Second Counts* (Broadway, 2003), he gives us the answer: "I've often said that cancer was the best thing that ever happened to me . . . the fact is that I wouldn't have won even a single Tour de France without the lesson of illness." Depending on how you choose to react to adversity, it can make you stronger and better, and you can make a comeback.

Approximately one year after our daughter's death, my wife and I decided to try and have another child. There were many complications, but two years later our family was truly blessed with the birth of a baby girl. At the same time, the company I was now president of was making its own comeback. Only seven months after our daughter was born, the company had its best year in its thirty-two-year history and we broke almost every sales record.

> **Things don't go wrong and break your heart so you can become bitter and give up. They happen to break you down and build you up so you can be all that you were intended to be.**
>
> **—Charlie "Tremendous" Jones, legendary author and speaker**

After the rain and the pain there will be brighter days. If you experience adversity in your life, look deep inside for strength and continue on. Always have faith in yourself. Accept your adversities and understand that they are preparing you for greater success. Remember that God's delays aren't necessarily God's denials.

Adversity doesn't have to be the beginning of the end. You gotta get past the starting line—or even the "restarting line"— if you're ever going to reach the finish line. It's no disgrace to start again. It can even be an opportunity to step back, evaluate your situation, and then reshape your dreams and goals.

Don't allow adversity to steal your dreams—don't even let it conceal your ultimate purpose. Instead, use adversity to reveal to you the inner resources you didn't even know you possessed. Use adversity to peel back your dreams to their foundations—to inspect them for flaws—and to rededicate yourself to making your dreams real.

Adversity is a testing of your mettle, your spirit, your character, and your courage. You can emerge either refined or resigned. You will have turning points—those forks in the road when the decisions you make will determine your ultimate destiny. Adversity can clarify your vision and reignite your purpose and passion. Or, it can give you the excuse you need to retire to the sidelines and seek the sympathies of all the others who are sitting on the bench.

To win, you gotta overcome adversity.

To overcome adversity, you gotta

- Know there will be big challenges
- Learn from your challenges
- Pick yourself up
- Make a comeback

Use adversity to peel back your dreams to their foundations—to inspect them for flaws—and to rededicate yourself to making your dreams real.

★ CHAPTER 12 ★

YOU GOTTA STAY IN TO WIN

WE'VE ALL HEARD the saying, "Winners never quit and quitters never win." If you're going to win, you gotta get in the game and you gotta stay in the game. True champions will stick it out through the ups and the downs, the good and the bad.

Many people believe you've got to be lucky to succeed. This is exactly the type of mediocre thinking that holds you back and keeps you from achieving your goals. Luck is hitting a jackpot in Las Vegas or winning the lottery. Luck is when something just falls in your lap. Success is doing what's right long enough until you finally achieve your goals. If you're betting on luck, good fortune, or your turn to win, you might hit the jackpot; then again, you might not. However, if you create your own luck, your odds of winning increase substantially.

There is only one recipe for creating luck, and it has two ingredients: hard work and determination. Some people define luck as an acronym: Laboring Under Correct Knowledge. But all the knowledge in the world won't do you any good without hard work and determination. I would say that luck is laboring, learning from your mistakes, making slight changes, and then pressing on.

> **Champions keep playing until they get it right.**
>
> **—Billie Jean King, hall of fame women's tennis champion**

To create your own luck, you must take action, do the work, and pay the price of success. Thomas Jefferson said it best: "I find that the harder I work, the more luck I seem to have."

Unfortunately, it's becoming more and more difficult to find people with the determination it takes to become an all-star. We live in a "microwave" society based on fast food and short marriages. Few people will stay in the game when times get tough. Your determination will come from staying

It's just an inescapable fact of life—if you want success, you gotta pay the price.

focused and persistent. Getting in the game is important, but staying in the game is the only way to win.

YOU GOTTA PAY THE PRICE

To succeed in athletics, sales, business, or anything else, you gotta pay the price. To get to the top and stay there takes years of hard work, dedication, and commitment. Too many people look at paying the price as a negative, but you should view it as a positive. If you pay the price of success today, you will enjoy the rewards and benefits in the future.

Pick any superstar athlete, and you can bet he paid a price for their success: years of daily practices; time in the game, time on the bench; losing seasons; blood, sweat, and tears—literally; missing out on fun and family time.

It's just an inescapable fact of life—if you want success, you gotta pay the price. Unfortunately, many people think high achievers just wake up one day to instant success. These people seem to ignore the case of the determined salesperson who makes call after call after call, only to receive voicemail messages, rudeness, and people who "forgot" he was coming. And he does the same thing day after day. These people think that winners have never worked for days to close a sale, only to have it canceled the next morning.

> **The difference between the impossible and the possible lies in a person's determination.**
>
> **—Tommy Lasorda, professional baseball hall of famer**

Everyone wants to make the game-winning shot. People want the rewards of being a sales leader, of rising through the ranks, of owning a successful business. But are they willing to put forth the effort to make it happen? Are they willing to show up every day ready to do what it takes? Are they willing to work twelve to sixteen hours a day, six to seven days a week to get there? Are they willing to pay the price of success?

One of my favorite quotes about paying the price is from motivational speaker Les Brown:

> If you want a thing bad enough to go out and fight for it, to work day and night for it, to give up your time, your peace, and your sleep for it . . . if all that you dream and scheme is about it, and life seems useless and worthless without it . . . if you gladly sweat for it and fret for it and plan for it and lose all your terror of the opposition for it . . . if you simply go after that thing you want with all of your capacity, strength and sagacity, faith, hope and confidence and stern pertinacity . . . if neither cold, poverty, famine, nor gaunt, sickness nor pain of body and brain, can keep you away from the thing that you want . . . if dogged and grim you beseech and beset it, with the help of God, you WILL get it! (Les Brown, *Live Your Dreams* [New York: HarperCollins], 130)

There are no shortcuts to success. It always comes with a price. You may love to play golf, go fishing, or watch TV, but you can't putt, cast, or be a couch potato all day and expect to achieve any true level of success.

YOU GOTTA STAY FOCUSED

If you're going to win the game, you gotta stay focused on your dreams and goals. It's a simple idea that's actually very difficult to practice. Why? Because any time you make a decision to do something, you're going to encounter distractions and obstacles. All sorts of resistance can and will show up to steal your time, your attention, and eventually your dreams if you let it. The challenge is to ignore the distractions, overcome the obstacles, and stay focused on the goal.

Distractions are probably your biggest opponent when it comes to achieving your goals. And interestingly, it's usually the small day-to-day diversions, those urgent but not important tasks, that are the most distracting. Most people spend too much time doing "second things" first. They get sidetracked, running here and there, confusing busyness with business. They do a thousand things, but they don't accomplish much. And when they do finally get around to working on their dreams and goals, they don't have enough energy or creativity left for the things that affect their lives the most. If your dreams and goals get the leftovers of your life, you'll never achieve them.

> **You must remain focused on your journey to greatness.**
>
> **—Les Brown, motivational speaker**

Stay focused by continually asking yourself, "Is what I'm doing moving me toward my goals and purpose? Or am I just spinning my wheels, being busy but not really making any progress?" Use your goals to guide you in prioritizing your time. Otherwise, you'll wander aimlessly through your days, doing whatever urgent tasks come up, instead of completing the steps necessary to move toward your goals.

Let me tell you a story. You may have heard it before, but its message is a good reminder no matter how many times you hear it.

One day, a professor was teaching a class about time management. The professor set a one-gallon glass jar on the table and filled it up with rocks. He asked the class, "Is this jar full?" Of course, the students said, "Yes!" Then he pulled out a bag of pebbles and poured them into the jar. As he did, he shook the jar so that the pebbles sifted down through the holes between the rocks. Eventually, the pebbles reached the top. Again, he asked the class, "Is this jar full?" The students cautiously answered, "Yes."

Next, he pulled out a bag of sand and did the same thing—pouring and shaking, until the sand reached the top of the jar. This time when he asked the class if the jar was full,

Always schedule those tasks that move you toward your goals first.

he got a resounding, "No!" Finally, he pulled out a pitcher of water and poured that into the jar until the water reached the top.

Every hour that passes is one less hour you have left to accomplish your dreams and goals.

Then he asked the students, "What was the point of this illustration?" One young man jumped up and said, "I know what it is: No matter how full your schedule is, if you try hard enough, you can always fit some more things into it!"

"No," the professor said, shaking his head. "You've missed the point. The truth this illustration teaches us is this: If you don't put the big rocks in first, you'll never get them in at all."

If you fill your jar with pebbles, sand, or water first, there will be no room for rocks. The less important things (the "second things") will take up all your time, and you won't ever get the big rocks (your dreams and goals) accomplished. Always schedule those tasks that move you toward your goals first. Once you schedule your goal-related activities, then you can fill in with all those other activities that are less important but still need accomplishing.

Studies have shown that you should give 80 percent of your time and attention to the top 20 percent of your priorities. That means you should spend 80 percent of your time on your dreams and goals, and 20 percent of your time on everything else. Do you put your rocks in your jar first, or do you fill your jar with all the little pebbles and sands of distraction?

Another effective strategy for staying focused is to delegate as many "second things" as possible. Most of us tend to think that nobody can do things as well as we can, so we end up doing it all. We spend our energy on activities that aren't the best use of our time and talents. Stop getting bogged down with all those things you know you shouldn't be involved with. Focus on your goals and be happy to delegate (and monitor) the rest.

We all have the same precious twenty-four hours each day. How you choose to use that time is vitally important. Every hour that passes is one less hour you have left to accomplish your dreams and goals. Are you investing your time or wasting it?

YOU GOTTA KEEP YOUR FIELD OF DREAMS GREEN

Throughout my career, I've learned to appreciate and understand the power of focus that high-performance people possess. The movers and shakers don't allow every good deal or pie-in-the-sky opportunity that comes along to distract them. They understand that if they're going to win, they have to continually focus on their own game, the game they've established for themselves.

Stop looking for something better and stay focused on the opportunity at hand.

I get emails, faxes, and phone calls every day from people trying to get me interested in different moneymaking deals. I never pursue any of them. People ask me if I feel like I may miss out on an opportunity. I tell them I don't know, but I don't have time to worry about it because I'm focused on becoming the best I can be with the fantastic opportunity I already have.

I have a friend who's always jumping from one opportunity or business to another. To him, the grass is always greener on another field. He's never learned that if you water and fertilize the grass on your own field, it will get greener and you'll want to stay. Sometimes the grass truly is greener somewhere else, but that's only because someone is over there taking care of it!

Take care of the grass on your own field. If you're convinced you've found your field of dreams, build it! Stop looking for something better and stay focused on the opportunity at hand. If you do, eventually it will become so fresh and desirable that others will want to play on your field.

YOU GOTTA BE PERSISTENT

Most superstars weren't always great, but they were persistent enough to stay in the game and keep improving until they achieved success. Persistence, or perseverance, means continuing in spite of opposition or discouragement.

George Foreman got back into boxing for one reason—to win the world championship. He had been retired from boxing for ten years when he put on his gloves again in 1987. He was considered the underdog in most fights: he was middle-aged, overweight, and out of shape. However, he knew that if he kept throwing the same punches consistently one of them would land on the right spot and win him the championship belt. No one expected him to win, but he had the dream and the goal and he believed he could win.

Foreman continued boxing and worked his way back to the top standing. And on November 6, 1994, his hard work paid off when he faced Michael Moorer in Las Vegas for the heavyweight title. Foreman was a 3–1 underdog, and at forty-five years old, many people didn't give him a chance against the twenty-six-year-old Moorer. But two minutes and ten seconds into the tenth round, he landed the famous right that sent Moorer down for the count. George Foreman reclaimed his world championship. He became the oldest heavyweight champ in boxing history because he kept on swinging.

When you have superstar persistence, you will consistently take action no matter what obstacles or challenges you may face; you will do whatever it takes to achieve your objective and claim victory. Perseverance is one of the key distinctions that separates the all-stars from the average in any situation.

Thomas Edison was an unbelievably prolific inventor. He holds more patents (1,093) than any other person in U.S. history. Did you know that Edison and his associates failed more than nine thousand times before finally discovering the secret to the light bulb? It takes amazing persistence to continue to shrug off that kind of failure!

> **Press on. Nothing in the world can take the place of persistence.**
> **—Ray Kroc, philanthropist and founder of McDonald's Corporation**

Colonel Sanders was told no more than a thousand times before he sold his first piece of Kentucky Fried Chicken. At the age of fifty-four, he drove from town to town, restaurant to restaurant, often sleeping in his car, believing his "secret recipe" would eventually pay off. Can you imagine the faith, patience, and perseverance it took for him to keep going?

A favorite saying in the sales profession is, "I've got to get my noes out of the way." I know a salesperson who got twenty-one noes in a row. He almost quit. Instead, he was persistent, and his twenty-second sales call was successful and launched his career. Three months later, he was a national sales champion, outselling every other salesperson in his company for that month.

Are you able to keep your mind engaged and persevere through your failures and the noes? Will you try to improve with every chance you're given? When you encounter a failure, don't beat yourself up. Do your best to learn from it, make adjustments, and continue to take action. Some things have to be learned from experience. Treat each failure as an opportunity to move closer to your goals. If Edison hadn't learned from his nine thousand failures and relentlessly persisted, we might all still be sitting in the dark.

Treat each failure as an opportunity to move closer to your goals.

The force behind some of history's boldest achievements is simply this: The diligent will to persevere. Sometimes we refer to this as sheer determination, or we say someone has lots of guts. It's all about staying power. It takes great persistence to continue believing in yourself in the face of failure. But don't give up! Keep on trying and you will eventually succeed. Never forget that every no is one step closer to a yes!

You gotta stay in to win.

To stay in to win, you gotta

- Pay the price
- Stay focused
- Keep your field of dreams green
- Be persistent

★ CONCLUSION ★

NO ONE, NOT EVEN the most amazing all-star, wins every single game. And rarely does a team have a perfect season. So just because you may lose a game here and there doesn't mean you're not a winner.

> If you can dream it, you can do it. Never lose sight of the fact that this whole thing was started by a mouse.
>
> —Walt Disney, visionary film producer and innovator in animation

Winning is really about the decisions you make, lessons you learn, and actions you take as you play the game. It's about developing your talents, stretching your abilities, and becoming more successful in many ways.

The truth is, if you're not progressing, you're moving backwards, especially in today's ever-changing world. There is no status quo. The key is to constantly strive for improvement. If you start to slip back, take action quickly to stop the slide, analyze the situation, and set a new course. Even if you have to take teeny-tiny steps at first, the smallest progress is far better than any movement backwards.

If you're going to be an all-star, you gotta get in the game, you gotta stay in the game, and you gotta follow the game plan. You already have all the talent and ability you need to win. But you gotta take action if you want to realize your goal of winning. Throughout this book, I've laid out a step-by-step plan that will virtually guarantee your success—if you put it into action.

The best part about winning is realizing that even when you do win, the game is not over. Instead, winning just means you can step back for a moment, enjoy the season, regenerate yourself, and start a new game with new goals and a different set of challenges. Success merely changes the game.

WHY NOT YOU?

It doesn't matter what happened yesterday or the day before or five minutes ago. You can't change the past. What you can do is change now, change tomorrow, change the next day, change the next month, and change the rest of your life.

> **You were born to win; but to be the winner you were born to be, you must plan to win and prepare to win. Then, and only then, can you legitimately expect to win.**
>
> **—Zig Ziglar, author and motivational speaker**

In the near future, new all-stars will emerge in your particular game. Some of them may even go on to nationwide fame. These all-stars will consistently take action and follow through with what they learn. Will you be one of them?

Don't be a spectator in the game. You can surface as a champion. You can live the life of your dreams. It's truly your choice. It all comes down to a decision, a clear unequivocal decision. You gotta decide today to do whatever it takes to get off the bench and become an all-star!

★ BONUS ★

YOU GOTTA HAVE
A DREAM BOOK

IF YOU'VE READ this far in the book, you know that dreams are absolutely critical to your success. But let's get down to the nitty-gritty. How can you effectively use dreams to truly achieve success? The following steps will show you how.

> Setting goals for your game is an art. The trick is in setting them at the right level—neither too low nor too high.
>
> —Greg Norman, PGA champion

STEP 1: YOU GOTTA INVEST SOME TIME

It takes time to properly set your goals. Only about 3 percent of people have ever clearly defined their goals in life. As a result, few will ever actually achieve their dreams. This is because they won't take the time to take the first step. So start immediately. You will have to invest some time, but this small investment of time will produce big payoffs in the future as your dreams become reality.

To start your Dream Book, all you need is a notebook and something to write with. Put this book down right now and go get them. You'll be glad you did.

STEP 2: YOU GOTTA MAKE A LIST OF ALL YOUR DREAMS

On the first page of the notebook, list everything you ever dreamed of having. Let your imagination go wild; write down everything you ever wanted. If you knew nothing was impossible, what would you attempt? Write it down on your list!

Remember to vividly describe your dreams when writing your list. Do not say, "I would like to make a lot of money every month." Instead, write down something like, "Beginning in January I will earn $10,000 per month."

Some things on the list should be big, long-term goals. Others should be medium term, two to five years out. Many will be smaller and shorter term, such as weekly, monthly, and yearly. You'll even want to have some ongoing daily goals. But regardless of the size or time frame, every goal should be specific.

When setting goals, concentrate on these categories to help you get started:

- Relationships
- Career
- Lifestyle
- Health and fitness
- Finances
- Mental and spiritual growth

Be sure to include items that are not necessarily materialistic. You could have a goal for helping others that says, "I will mentor at least one new employee for three months each year." Or you could have a relationship goal that states, "I will spend three hours a week with my spouse, just the two of us." Think of anything and everything that will make you feel happier and more successful.

In the following steps, you'll refine your list, but this step is a "sky's the limit" exercise. You are limited only by your own imagination.

STEP 3: YOU GOTTA DECIDE IF IT'S TRULY IMPORTANT

Now, go back and reread each item you listed and ask yourself these three questions about each one:

1. Is this really my dream?
2. Can I see myself reaching it?
3. Will achieving it benefit my life and the lives of those around me (for example, my family)?

If you can answer yes to all three questions, keep the item on your list. But if you cannot answer yes to every question, then cross the dream off your list. By the time you reach the end of the list, you will have discovered what matters most in your life!

STEP 4: YOU GOTTA KNOW THE WHYS

Now turn to the next blank page in the notebook and make three categories for establishing goals: short-term (up to two years), medium-term (two to five years), and long-term (more than five years). Transfer your most important goals (the ones you answered yes to for all three questions) to this page, placing them in the appropriate category—short-, medium- or long-term. Be sure to leave some blank space by each goal.

Don't make the list too long—ten or fifteen goals are plenty to get you started. Try to make sure that you have approximately the same number of goals in each category.

Next, in the blank space, write down why you must achieve each goal. You gotta know the "whys" behind your goals because that's what will get you up early and keep you up late. The whys will give you the burning desire and passion that will see you through the tough times to your ultimate victory.

> **Those who only know the hows always end up working for those who know the whys.**
>
> **—Bryan Dodge, author and motivational speaker**

If you can't write down why you want to achieve an item on your list, then it is not a real goal. Cross it off your list!

STEP 5: YOU GOTTA BUILD THE DREAM

Next, make a separate page for each of your most important goals—the ones where you were able to write down a "why." Write each goal at the top of the page.

Now you are going to expand and build your dreams by finding pictures of each of your goals. As you find pictures, place them on the applicable page in your Dream Book. Draw the pictures yourself if you have to. Remember, these pictures will help you visualize your goals. It's not an art contest. It's a mental exercise that will change your life.

Pictures that include you will work best. For example, if your goal is to have a new Cadillac, any picture of a Cadillac will do. But if you can take a picture of yourself with the specific Cadillac in the color you want, it will work better.

Some of your goals will include intangible items for which you can't easily get pictures. For these items, use something visual that represents and relates to the dream or goal. (You may have to get creative!) Perhaps your goal is to earn twice what you're making now. You could use your pay stub, mark out the amount, and write in the amount you want it to be.

> **The moment of enlightenment is when a person's dreams of possibilities become images of probabilities.**
>
> **—Vic Braden, professional tennis player**

Follow through until you have pictures for as many of your primary goals as you can. Next, below the picture for each goal, write two questions and leave space for the answers:

1. What action steps am I willing to take to achieve this goal?
2. What sacrifices am I willing to make to achieve this goal?

Now go back and answer the two questions under each goal, taking the time to give your answers some serious thought.

Keep in mind that anything worthwhile requires sacrifice, whether it's time, money, or the pursuit of other goals. We all make sacrifices every single day. Sometimes they're the wrong kind, like sacrificing your standards to make a quick buck. The wrong kind of sacrifices will hold you back in your pursuit of your dreams and goals. But if you choose to make the right kinds of sacrifices for a valuable purpose, you will propel yourself toward your goals.

STEP 6: YOU GOTTA MAKE YOUR DREAMS REAL

If you've gotten this far, you are well on your way to achieving your dreams. But there's still another critical step: You gotta make your dreams real. You gotta go out and see, touch, and experience as many of the dreams you've listed as you can.

If you want a new house, find a house like the one you want and take some pictures of your family in front of it. Walk through it and see, touch, and smell the inside of it. If it's a new car you want, go to the car dealership and pick out the color and options you want and test-drive the car.

Experiencing your dreams and goals like this makes them real for you in a way that no picture can. It shows you what your life will be like when you achieve your goals. Once you've physically experienced a goal, every time you see the picture of that goal in your dream book, you will remember what it was like to live that goal, and you'll increase your burning desire to accomplish it.

STEP 7: YOU GOTTA CLAIM VICTORY

Finally, as you begin to work toward each goal, be sure to write down the date you start. And as you accomplish each of your goals, use a red pen and write the word "Victory!" over the goal. As you flip through your Dream Book and see all the "victory pages," it will become a tremendous motivator because it will let you know you are winning the game.

But don't stop just because you achieve the original goals you write down in your dream book. One of the biggest mistakes I've seen over the years with the thousands of people who have used the dream book is that once they hit their initial goals, they don't set new, bigger goals.

Once you follow these steps and set your first goals, you will know how to set and achieve all your subsequent goals and you will begin to realize your dreams. Your first dream book will take you as far as you can see, and when you get there you will see farther still. Then it's time to set some new goals!

To be an all-star, you gotta have a dream book.

To create a dream book, you gotta

- Invest some time
- Make a list of all your dreams
- Decide if it's truly important
- Know the whys
- Build the dream
- Make your dreams real
- Claim victory

ACKNOWLEDGMENTS

AS WITH ANYTHING of significance, the completion of this book involved a great team.

I want to start by thanking Lisa O'Dell, Larry Liner, and Bill Osborn—without your input, help, ideas, and research, this book would not be the same. To Nancy Angelo, thank you for your patience, understanding, and the time you graciously gave to help with this project; I couldn't have done it without you. I wish to thank Bryan Dodge for your review of this book, the encouragement you've given me, and for introducing me to David Cottrell and Cornerstone Leadership; you truly helped make this dream a reality. To my friend and neighbor Kent Barry, I owe you a debt of gratitude for the time and effort you volunteered and the input you've given to make this book possible.

To Juli Baldwin, Laurie Magers, and Luis Escalante, thank you for the extra work you have given this project. To the team at Greenleaf Book Group, especially Lari Bishop, Jay Hodges, and Sheila Parr, thanks for the excellent work and creative ideas to make *The All-Star Sales Book* possible.

A very special thank you to Ray and Toni Jones and the Jones family for giving me the opportunity to run your company. My heartfelt thanks go to: Bill and Lara Kellett, Gene and Daune Melvin, Jack and Arlene Mohler, Tom and Alice Cardy, Craig and Julie Schwienebart, Gene and Carolyn Shelton, Larry and Patty Smith, Dale and Lois Archer, Dale and Deborah Ruschy, Justin and Sharon Wolbers, Ron and Lisa Reed, Zane and Heidi Gray, Darin and Marianne Kendrick, Jeff and Susan Lamb, and Marco and Deborah Gonzalez.

To A. V. and Wanda Holden, thank you for always being fair and for being like second parents to Susan and me. Thanks to Gene Shelton for recruiting me into sales. Thanks also to Mickey Frye for teaching us that every day can be a payday and a holiday. My appreciation to Kim Havens for being organized enough for all of us. And to Chris and Becky Roberts, my deepest gratitude for your tremendous support over the years and for everything you have contributed to our lives and our business. Deserving of special attention are James and Cindy Wilkerson for always being there and for stepping up and helping out when we needed you the most. Mostly, my thanks go to every single member of our team for making our mission possible.

To Zig Ziglar, you have been an inspiration to me since I was just a kid. I am grateful to John Maxwell, Jim Rohn, Tony Jeary, Les Brown, Ed Young Jr., Jim Madrid, and Joel Osteen for your positive influence on my life.

I especially want to thank my friend and mentor Charlie "Tremendous" Jones. You are one of the greatest men I have ever met.

Finally, I want to give special thanks to my family. To my mother, Mary Updegrove, and father, Eugene Cox, without your guidance in my life there is no telling where I might be. Thanks also to my sisters Shirley, Deborah, Sherry, and Candy. To my grandmother, Nelly Cox, I hope I am still in the game, like you are, when I am eighty-seven.

To my children—Blake, Chase, Connor, and Destany—you are the greatest kids in the world. Life has something special in store for each of you. Remember that the sky is the limit. To my daughter Skylar, you are an angel. God chose you to go to Heaven, and I know we will see you again someday.

And to my wife, Susan, thank you for being patient and allowing me to burn the midnight oil to complete this book. But most of all, thank you for just being who you are; for sharing your life, love, and dreams with me; and for the support you've always given me even when I didn't deserve it. I would have never become the person I am today without your love and support.

ABOUT THE AUTHOR

FOR NEARLY TWO DECADES, Billy Cox has dedicated his life to helping others achieve their dreams. He is a leading authority on sales excellence and an expert in helping individuals and organizations achieve peak performance. Billy started in sales and marketing when he was just seventeen years old. Over a period of fifteen years, he worked his way to the top of his organization. By age thirty Billy was a self-made millionaire. At age thirty-two he became president of an international sales and marketing company. When he took over as president, sales were down 50 percent from their all-time highs. Working as a team, Billy and the other company leaders used the powerful concepts and techniques presented in this book to achieve record sales in only two and a half years.

Billy is a "no limits" person who knows how to win. His hands-on experience and proven track record make him one of the best success coaches in America today. He is a master salesman, a compelling motivator, and an energetic leader who believes that if you're going to win, you gotta get in the game!

Billy considers his personal accomplishments to be just as important as his professional achievements. He regularly donates his time and talents to youth sports, community service work, and various charities. Billy lives in the suburbs of Dallas, Texas, with his wife, Susan, and their four children.

HOW TO HELP YOUR TEAM
BECOME ALL-STARS

Keynote Presentations

Let author Billy Cox personally inspire and empower your organization, team, or conference attendees. A keynote with Billy is truly a learning experience that is motivational, interactive, fun, and specifically targeted to generate excitement, shift attitudes, and maximize performance.

Workshops

Facilitated by a certified instructor, this three- or six-hour foundation-building program will show every team member, new or experienced, how to apply the all-star concepts and strategies. These workshops are highly interactive and customized to your team's environment and challenges.

"Get in the Game" PowerPoint Presentation ($99.95)

You can introduce and reinforce the Get in the Game concept in your organization with this easy-to-use, cost-effective presentation tool. All the key concepts and ideas from the book are highlighted in this professionally produced, downloadable PowerPoint presentation that includes a facilitator guide and notes. Use the presentation for kick-off meetings, training sessions, or as a follow-up developmental tool.

"You Gotta Get in the Game" Audio CD Set ($19.95)

Many people won't take the time to read an entire book, but they will listen to an audio program. This unabridged version of the book includes bonus material from author Billy Cox not included in the book.

"Playing in the Majors" Audio CD ($9.95)

This audio program will teach your team how to stay focused on high-impact activities and how to quit majoring in the minor tasks that don't contribute to long-term success.

Free Get in the Game Tools

Log on to www.ChampionshipSales.com for free tools to help you get in the game, stay in the game, and win!

"The Dream Book: Seven Steps to Change Your Life" ($14.95)

If you've ever dreamed of a better life, The Dream Book will teach you how to achieve the extraordinary life you desire and deserve. The Dream Book is a revolutionary technology for goal design and personal achievement. It will guide you through a seven-step process to change any area of life or business that you desire.

"Making the Dream Book Work" Audio CD Set ($19.95)

No matter what your dreams, you can achieve them if you will follow the simple steps outlined on this audio. This CD set will share with you the power of dreams. Put yourself on the fast track to living your dreams today!

For more information on keynotes and workshops or to order products, contact us at

www.ChampionshipSales.com
1.800.722.4685, 1.972.899.2458
Email: info@ChampionshipSales.com

INDEX